At Christ's Table

At Christ's Table

MEDITATIONS AND PRAYERS FOR COMMUNION

edited by
Dorothy D. France

Chalice Press
St. Louis, Missouri

Biblical quotations, unless otherwise noted, are from the *New Revised Standard Version Bible*, copyright 1989, Division of Christian Education of the National Council of the Churches of Christ in the USA. Used by permission.

Those quotations marked RSV are from the *Revised Standard Version* of the Bible, copyrighted 1946, 1952, © 1971, 1973.

"On Pentecost They Gathered," © 1981, reprinted by permission of Jane Parker Huber.

Cover design: Chris Vculek

10 9 8 7 6 5 4 3 2   97 98 99 00 01 02

Library of Congress Cataloging–in–Publication Data

At Christ's table :   meditations and prayers for communion / Dorothy D. France, editor.
    p.   cm.
    Includes bibliographical references and index.
    ISBN 0-8272-0022-6
    1. Lord's Supper (Liturgy)—Texts.   2. Christian Church (Disciples of Christ)—Liturgy—Texts.   3. Eucharistic prayers—Christian Church (Disciples of Christ).   4. Christian Church (Disciples of Christ)—Prayer-books and devotions—English.   5. Lord's Supper—Christian Church (Disciples of Christ).   I. France, Dorothy D.
BX7325.5.L67A7   1997   96-6588
   264'.0663—dc21   CIP

Printed in the United States of America

CONTENTS

INTRODUCTION

Dorothy D. France

When I was a very young child, I knew that there was something very special about that "large wooden table" that stood in center front of the place where we gathered for the opening of Sunday school and church. Each Sunday as the children and adults left the Sunday school "opening exercises" for our classrooms, I would see several women going to that table with white cloths and some special trays. They would cover the table with one of the cloths, making sure it was placed just right. Then they sat two trays that contained crackers and juice in a certain spot on that table. When everything was just the way they wanted it, they covered the trays with the other white cloth. It was done the same way every Sunday. Even when different women did it, it was always handled the same. I knew just how it was done because sometimes I stopped on my way to class to watch them.

On certain Sundays I knew my dad would stand beside that table and after saying a prayer, out loud so all could hear him, he would pick up the trays one at a time and hand them to the others who had come to the table to help him. The helpers—I learned later that they were called "deacons"—would then leave the table and walk up and down the space between the seats passing those "refreshments" to the older children and adults. I was always told that when I was older I would understand.

1

It wasn't until much later that I really understood what it was all about, but I always knew it was special. When my dad stood at that table I was so proud. He would be dressed in his neatly pressed suit with a white shirt starched just right, and he always wore his best tie. He wore a white flower pinned on his suit coat. This was a time of quietness and prayer. Occasionally the silence would be broken by the sound of the cups being placed back in the tray or by a cough or sneeze that just couldn't be stifled.

In recent years as I have joined in worship in many of our churches in various locations, I have often longed for that special quiet time about the table. Somehow it seems to have lost some of its importance or specialness to church members that it once had. In our effort to make everyone comfortable and at ease, we seem to have compromised its sacredness and meaning. I sense on some Sunday mornings that things must be hurried along as the noon hour approaches. If things are running late, the easiest thing to shorten appears to be the time about the table. I've heard comments after the benediction such as, "We're late getting out this morning. Let's hurry or we'll have to stand in line to get a table ahead of the members of the church down the street." We rush from the most sacred table of all to fulfill our physical passion for food about other tables.

Oh, I'm not minimizing the importance of gathering about tables. It was, after all, about a dinner table that the Lord's supper was instituted. But I do sense that something is being lost in the hurriedness of our lives. I know that many persons have sensed this, too, because they have expressed their concern regarding the casualness with which we approach the table. Many have asked why so little guidance is provided for new Christians regarding the centrality of the Lord's supper for Disciples and why, when they are asked to serve, little or no real preparation and training is provided. However, I realize that many of our churches do an excellent job with training and preparation and commend them for it.

But I still have to ask the question: Has the coming about Christ's table become so routine that we take it for granted? Have we conditioned ourselves into thinking that everyone knows and will always know how to prepare, care for, and serve in the place where Jesus himself served about the table?

At Christ's Table comes in response to a request initially made some years ago by Mary Lou Williams, an elder in the West Side Christian Church, Portsmouth, Virginia. Since that time many others have asked for help and suggested that now would be a good time for me to spend some retirement time pulling resources together that they could have in one guidebook. I express my gratitude to them for their persistence and to all those who have so willingly contributed to this publication. It is my prayer that those children, and perhaps some adults as well, who are waiting in the wings and observing our behavior, will catch from our example the real significance of the Master's words, "Do this in remembrance of me," and join us as "at Christ's table" we celebrate.

+ + +

Larry Hastings has written movingly of the communion chalice that has become a symbol of our identity, and which graces the headings in this book. Ponder his words:

The symbol of the Christian Church (Disciples of Christ)
    is both very simple and very profound.
A cup, a chalice, a cross,
A living reminder of Christ,
    of his cup, his chalice, his cross.
It is known by many different names:
    the holy eucharist, the Lord's Supper, communion.
Whatever name we call it, it means the same thing,
    expressed in many different ways:
His body broken for us, his love poured out for us,
    his life, always present for us.

We commune every week
    as the fundamental expression of who we are:
        the symbol of our community,
        the expression of our oneness
        with God and with each other.
Christian unity is the focal point,
Christian unity is the core,
Christian unity is the heart
        of our denomination's origins,
        of our church's history,
        and of our present identity.
Our unity is our witness for Christ,
Our unity is our message of love,
Our unity is our mission to our divided world.

We do not stress one narrow set of doctrines,
        because doctrines, as instructive as they are,
    do not make us one.
We do not emphasize one single system of beliefs,
    because beliefs, as essential as they are,
    do not make us one.
We do not acknowledge one bishop or prelate over us,
    because human authorities, as powerful as they are,
    do not make us one.

We emphasize communion with Christ
    because Christ and Christ alone,
    makes us one.
His table is the center of our sanctuary.
His cross is the center of our lives.
His cup is the nourishment of our hungry hearts.
His communion with us
    empowers us
    to live as his communion cup
    pouring out our lives
    on behalf of the world.

DISCIPLES OF CHRIST AND THE LORD'S TABLE

Peter M. Morgan

The Christian Church was conceived at the Lord's table at Barton W. Stone's Cane Ridge meeting house in 1801. The Lord's supper at Cane Ridge? Fiery preaching, yes! Spirit-filled exercises of barks, jerks, "deep" singing, yes! An ecumenical gathering that melted denominational antagonisms, yes! Few of us know, however, that the Cane Ridge, Kentucky, Revival of August 1801 was an American frontier version of a Scottish Presbyterian "Holy Fair." The Cane Ridge Revival continued that practice of persons from more than one congregation gathering for an evangelistic and eucharistic occasion. We were conceived at the Lord's table.

Our church's faith was formed at the Lord's table. We continue to believe and celebrate as a people of the table. In our time each Disciples congregation assembles every week to break the loaf and to share the cup in a way similar to the way we have done it for most of our history. In that practice we see the defining characteristics of the Christian Church (Disciples of Christ).

We are a biblical people. The Gospels tell of Jesus in the Upper Room sharing this special meal with his disciples. In the letters of the early church we read of their continuing to observe Jesus' command to break bread and pour wine as they remember him. The Disciples early leader, Alexander Campbell, identified this biblical command as one of the many "ordinances"

5

we are to obey in our practice of worship. Ordinances are God's gifts for bestowing grace: "all the wisdom, power, love, mercy, compassion, or grace of God is in the ordinances of the Kindgom of Heaven." The visionary Thomas Campbell, Alexander's father, was even more adamant: "New Testament worship ceases when the Lord's Supper is not observed every Lord's Day."

Our founders insisted that our church's faith and practice come from the New Testament. Thus, each week we gather at the table to say and to hear the words spoken by Jesus and to dine with Christ in the way he dined with his friends on the night he was betrayed.

We are a priestly people. Christ's ministry is given to the whole community of believers. We call on special spiritual leaders, pastors and elders, to lead us in this highest moment of our lives. Elders and pastors share at the table and thereby witness to the communal character of Christ's ministry. Their prayers and actions of service are then picked up and continued in the priestly work of the entire assembly as each person prays silently and as he or she serves the bread and wine to his or her neighbor in the pew. In the course of the meal, the sanctuary becomes a room filled with priests. We are a priestly people in prayer and service. All believers are priests.

We are a free church people. We recite no prescribed prayers at the table. Prayer books are useful aids to our prayer, not authoritative documents. Our practice is not governed by councils or synods. We are a free but responsible eucharistic community.

Our hero stories witness to our commitment to freedom. Young Alexander Campbell had passed the requirements to approach the table. When his turn came he simply left the admission token on the table and turned away unfed. Christ is the host. Who are we to keep anyone away?

Thomas Campbell received the censure of his Presbyterian Synod because he dared invite to Christ's table persons who were not of the specific branch of his denominational family. Christ is the host. Who are we to keep anyone away?

We are a free people who conform not to the authority of ecclesial councils but to the power of God's spirit, known in the mutual desire to come willingly and regularly into the presence of Christ at the table.

We are a Christ-centered people. Walter Scott, our great early evangelist, preached that Christ was the heart of the whole gospel message. Scott preached Christ, "The Golden Oracle."

We are a believing people. The great biblical themes of creation, redemption, salvation, covenant, eternal life, etc., are crucial to our thought, our education, our prayer, our witness, our service. Yet only one creed is essential to be a part of us. We confess with Peter, "You are the Christ."

At the table we come to commune intimately with the one at the heart of our faith, the heart of our lives. Alexander Campbell helps describe the powerful, personal encounter we experience with Christ at the table. "To every disciple he says, 'for you my body was wounded; for you my life was taken.' In receiving it the disciple says, 'Lord, I believe it. My life sprang from thy suffering; my joy from thy sorrow; my hope of glory everlasting from thy humiliation and abasement even to death.'"

We the people of the table have been transformed by our intimacy with Christ. We now turn to be in union, communion, with our brothers and sisters in Christ. With Campbell we say to others at the table, "You have owned my Lord as your Lord; my people are your people. Under Jesus the Messiah we are one. Mutually embraced in the everlasting arms, I embrace you in mine." The center of the life of our people is the table where we come together to be embraced by Christ and to embrace each other.

From Cane Ridge, Kentucky, 1801, on through two centuries of our history we celebrate who we are, Christ's people of the Chalice. We celebrate expectantly our place in Christ's ministry as those who prepare his table and say in his name to a hungry world, "Come!"

PREPARING TO CELEBRATE

Dorothy D. France

THE SERVICE

The Christian Church (Disciples of Christ) has made the Lord's supper the central element of worship by consistently celebrating it every Sunday. The communion table itself is the focal point in the sanctuary, reminding those who enter of the important role it plays in their spiritual life.

The worshiper must always be prepared before coming about the table. We commit a grave injustice to individuals when we assume that they will always be spiritually and physically ready to partake at any given moment. The service should be planned and conducted in such a manner that each person may be guided into a creative period of personal meditation and prayer. Time should be given for self-examination and the personal offering of one's life in renewed commitment. This cannot take place if the service is hurried or conducted as if it operated on a timer.

In most cases it is the minister, lay leader, or sometimes one of the elders who is given the responsibility of preparing the worshiper through the use of a meditation or call to communion. Regardless of what goes before, what comes after, or where it is located in the order of worship, the time about the table should always be entered into in celebration but with reverence, thoughtfulness, and thanksgiving. After all, the peak

9

experience of feeling one's self near to God comes as one partakes of the holy supper.

The procedure used in conducting the communion service itself may vary but the mechanics and differing customs do not alter in the least its true meaning. Some place the observance of the supper in the central part of the worship service; others have it following the sermon.

The elements are usually blessed by the minister or elder and passed among the congregation by members of the diaconate. In some congregations a whole loaf of bread is used along with individual wafers. Following the meditation or call to communion, the presiding minister or elder breaks the loaf, and while using Jesus' words, *"This is my body that is for you"* (1 Corinthians 11:24), holds the broken pieces up for all to see. A portion is then placed on each bread tray along with the other wafers. By the same token, the minister or presiding elder holds up the cup and again speaks the words of Jesus, *"This is my blood of the covenant, which is poured out for many for the forgiveness of sins"* (Matthew 26:28). The prayers for the bread and cup are then offered, and the plates and trays are distributed to the diaconate, who then serve the elements to those present.

In some congregations, the procedure known as *individual participation* is practiced. The plates of bread and trays of cups are distributed to individuals as they sit in the pew. When the plate is received, the bread or wafer is taken and eaten, and the plate is passed to the nearest person, who does likewise. The tray containing the cups is passed with each person removing a cup, drinking from it, replacing the drained cup into the tray, and passing it to the neighbor.

Other congregations practice what is known as *simultaneous participation*. The plates of bread are distributed first. After taking a bit of bread or a wafer, it is held while the plate is passed to the nearest neighbor. After all have been served, the presiding minister or elder invites participation, and all partake at the same time. The procedure is similar with the cup. The individual cup is removed from the tray, and the tray is then passed to the nearest person. The cup is held until all are invited to participate. The empty cup is then placed in a receptacle for that purpose located on the back of the pew. Sometimes the procedure may be combined, in which case the bread is eaten as passed and the cup held until all have been served and invited to partake by the presiding minister or elder.

On special days such as Christmas Eve, New Year's Eve, Maundy Thursday, or World Communion Sunday, individuals may be invited to come to the table, where they are served the bread and cup while kneeling at the altar or standing before the table. On such occasions, at the direction of an usher or other designated person, individuals sitting in the pew go forward and kneel or stand at a designated location. They are served the bread and cup and then directed back to their places in the congregation, where they continue in silent reflection while others are being served.

Many congregations provide communion on a regular basis to members who are homebound or living in retirement or nursing homes. They make sure that all are served each month, with the elders who serve for the Sunday morning service taking the communion to disignated individuals that afternoon. Other churches calendar this into the church schedule so all can receive the communion on the same Sunday of the month. That way individuals know when they will be visited. This is often the highlight of the month for many elders and shut-ins.

Guidelines are provided for those serving communion to the sick and homebound in the section "Communion in Special Settings."

Christ's presence is with us thoughout each communion gathering. We are reminded that he met and shared a meal with all his disciples—even the ones who betrayed him, denied him, and doubted him. When conducted and entered into with reverence and expectancy, the Lord's supper can be a breathtaking drama. May this be true each time we gather in his name.

THE SETTING

Familiarity often causes us to become careless about how we care for things, both in our homes and in the church. For the Disciples, the Lord's table has always had a permanent place in the house of worship and a central place in the worship experience. Having the table always before us may cause us to become careless about its care and the respect we give to it. The communion table is not the place around which we would ordinarily conduct a business meeting, store our coats and hats while we have choir practice, or carry on children's play activities.

On very special occasions the table often becomes the focal point for the placement of religious symbols, floral designs such as a cornucopia filled with fruits of the harvest, and other appropriate worship aides related to a special event being held in the sanctuary when communion is not to be received. Whenever this is done, one must remember the sacredness of the table and not let it become a replacement for a more appropriate table for "non-supper" events.

In most congregations the oversight of the preparation of the table and the service itself is assigned to the worship department or is the responsibility of the diaconate or other designated group. In many churches these persons are responsible for seeing that the grape juice and bread are purchased and readily available. Consideration should be given to the makeup of the congregation when selecting the bread to be used. Older persons and others with even minor handicaps may have difficulty picking up and handling the small piece of rectangular bread. Some congregations also include the wafer and a cube of bread on the tray to accommodate the needs of all those participating.

In churches where paraments are used, it is often these same individuals who are responsible for seeing that the paraments are changed to reflect the proper color for the season and that the table and chairs are clean—no dust or cobwebs please. They are also responsible for seeing that the communion ware is clean and properly placed on the table. It would be thoughtful to provide polishing cloths, cleaning products, and other materials which may be needed in removing spills and last minute fingerprints.

It is important that those persons assigned this important and sacred task know who they are and be given a written listing of their responsibilities. A schedule should be provided on a regular basis with a copy given to each person listed. It should also be posted in an appropriate location for quick reference. This should list those responsible for the actual preparation of the elements as well as those scheduled to serve on a given Sunday. The schedule for taking communion to the homebound or those in retirement or nursing homes should also be included so that everyone is aware of their particular duties.

Those preparing the table for the congregational setting may also be asked to prepare the emblems for use in the home or other setting. A portable communion kit is needed for this purpose and, if not already available, may be purchased from Christian Board of Publication.

The same respectful attention that is given in preparing the table and the elements before the worship service begins must be given to their removal following the benediction. Whenever possible they should be taken from the table to a designated area where the unused elements are properly handled, the trays are cleaned, and any linens that may need care before the next service are given proper care by those who have accepted this responsibility. Proper respect for the table warrants clean, white linen every time we gather.

THE SERVANT

"To an outsider one of the strangest Disciples customs is our designating laypersons to pray at the Lord's supper," states Colbert S. Cartwright in his book *People of the Chalice.* "In nearly all church bodies beyond our denomination the act of consecrating the communion elements is reserved for the clergy. They gain this exclusive privilege at the time of ordination." "Within the Disciples," Cartwright continues,

> elders are chosen to offer the prayers of thanksgiving at the table. An elder is not just another member of the congregation. Elders are thoughtfully and prayerfully selected to fulfill specific ministerial responsibilities. Since our beginning on the American frontier in the early 1800s and throughout all the changes of time, place, and circumstance since those frontier days, the responsibility and tasks of the Disciples elders have changed, but their place at the Lord's table has remained the same.[+]

The servants must be prepared to serve. It is recommended that an orientation or training session be held at least once a year for the elders and all members of the diaconate. These sessions are usually led by the minister or in some instances by the worship department or other designated person(s) and should include instruction in the proper handling of the trays and distribution of the elements, and some guidance in handling unusual situations, such as serving the bread and cup to handicapped or elderly persons who may need extra assistance. In some localities several congregations may choose to have joint training sessions, with the leadership and location for the sessions rotating each year.

No one may notice that the training has been provided because everything will run smoothly and reverently. They will surely notice, however, that it was not offered or taken advantage of, when their time of personal meditation has been unnecessarily disturbed. Last-minute recruiting of elders or members of the diaconate from the pews should be avoided as much as possible. Planning ahead for necessary substitutions will enable everyone to be at the proper place before the worship service begins.

[+]Colbert S. Cartwright, *People of the Chalice* (St. Louis: CBP Press, 1987), pp. 37-38.

Elders may need guidance in the preparation of their prayers. The prayers should be brief and in simple language. It is a real temptation to make them pastoral prayers rather than prayers of thanksgiving for the bread and the cup. Some may need to have them written and may find suggestions helpful regarding the use of "cue cards," e.g., taking them out of their pocket before coming to the table or placing them on the table before the worship service begins. Some may not be used to speaking in public and may need suggestions as to how to project their voices so they may be heard. Practicing alone or with a friend in the sanctuary may help new elders build confidence and become more at ease in the offering of the prayers.

The mechanics of how those serving approach the table may vary from congregation to congregation. In some churches the minister, elders, and members of the diaconate process with the choir into the sanctuary, where they take their places. Some prefer to have the elders and diaconate seated at the front of the congregation, some choose to have them seated at the rear, and still others prefer to have them seated with their families until the communion hymn is sung, at which time they come forward and take their places at the table.

The persons presiding at the Lord's table—minister , elders, and the members of the diaconate—all set the mood for the observance the moment that they begin to move from their seats and approach the table. Their demeanor should always be reverent and respectful, with each person knowing exactly where he or she is supposed to be and exactly what he or she is expected to do. This can and will not happen unless they have been given training and guidance before the worship service begins.

Those serving should dress for the occasion. Someone has aptly stated that "communion is best when we wear servants' clothing." When one is invited to a banquet or as a guest for a special celebration or event, one tries to dress in appropriate and respectful attire. Sometimes what is acceptable for one occasion may be less acceptable for another. Appropriate dress for men usually means a suit or jacket with tie; for women a dress, jacket dress, or suit would be considered in good taste. Bright colors and designs are great but in their proper place. Women should refrain from wearing dangling or loose fitting bracelets that might jingle or clang against the trays. Jewelry that might glitter when it catches the light perhaps should be saved for use on other occasions. Men should try to keep their hands out of their pockets, lest they be tempted to jingle their change, which would be best left to another time and place.

These guidelines are not meant to exclude anyone who might otherwise be able to serve. There are always exceptions and adjustments that should and must be made as the situation dictates. What one needs to remember is that those presiding and serving at the table are set apart. They now stand where Jesus stood, "to do what he did the night of his betrayal."

In some congregations the minister and the elders who are serving on that particular morning meet for a time of quietness and prayer prior to entering the sanctuary. This may be time well spent in seeking both mental and spiritual preparation. To prepare to "celebrate" is as serious as to prepare to deliver the word of God!

COMMUNION IN SPECIAL SETTINGS

Guidance and Meditations

The church's ministry to the sick is an immediate response to Jesus himself, whose mission to proclaim the kingdom of God was characterized by his healing ministry. "That evening, at sundown, they brought to him all who were sick....And the whole city was gathered around the door. And he cured many who were sick with various diseases." (Mark 1:32–34.)

Compassionate caring, to the early disciples, was consistent with that of Jesus. They had observed that when Jesus felt compassion for others he always followed with action. He visited with the sick, the handicapped, those who were suffering, and ministered to their need. "But Peter said, 'I have no silver or gold, but what I have I give you; in the name of Jesus Christ of Nazareth, stand up and walk.' And he took him by the right hand and raised him up." (Acts 3:6–7.)

It is this same sense of compassion for suffering that motivated the early church to care for the sick. "Are any among you sick? They should call for the elders of the church and have them pray over them." (James 5:14.)

The material is this section was prepared following consultation with two directors of pastoral care in the Richmond, Virginia, area. Appreciation is expressed to the Rev. Thomas Clements, Henrico Doctors Hospital, and the Rev. Robert Muncy, Richmond Memorial Hospital, for their time and excellent suggestions.

As we share in communion and fellowship with the sick or those handicapped in any way—whether in their homes, a nursing facility, or a hospital—we do so as an extension of the congregational celebration. We come as representatives of the family of God, individuals who want to understand and give support and encouragement.

It is important that time be taken to offer prayers of intercession for the person or persons to be visited and to pray that those who serve may be instruments of God's compassion and peace.

Thought also needs to be given beforehand to the "communion setting" itself. In addition to taking the bread and the cup, which are usually placed in containers provided in portable communion kits, take along a small white cloth—a white napkin also will work fine.

Following a brief visit, the transition to the communion service itself may be made as the setting is prepared. Lay the cloth or napkin on the tray table or other appropriate place which has been cleared as much as possible of medical paraphernalia, toiletries and so forth. Prepare and place the emblems on the cloth, and the brief service is ready to begin.

The material in the section "Retirement Community or Nursing Home" basically addresses communion in a group setting. For individuals who are confined to their rooms or to a special unit, the material in the "Private Residence" or "Hospital" setting may be useful. As an additional resource, see "An Order for the Lord's Supper with Those Confined" in *Chalice Hymnal*, pp. 769-70.

PRIVATE RESIDENCE

Someone has said that the "church is where we are." This is certainly true for persons who are "shut-in" or homebound. Individuals may be confined to their homes for various reasons. One may be caring for a spouse or child. Another may be crippled from arthiritis or suffering from another debilitating disease which makes getting in and out of a car or navigating stairs difficult or impossible. Another may have a terminal illness or be recovering from surgery. Others may be homebound for reasons that have not been made known. Whatever the reason, individuals confined close to home, as well as those who may care for them, need the love and support of their extended family—the church.

As they are visited and as the minister and elders gather with them from time to time about the Lord's table, they are reminded once again of God's presence in their lives and of the church as it gathers in their home.

The following are provided as seed thoughts for brief meditations, along with words of institution and a brief prayer for bread and cup. Other prayers from this book may be substituted where appropriate.

SCRIPTURE AND MEDITATION

"As soon as they left the synagogue, they entered the house of Simon and Andrew, with James and John." (Mark 1:29.)

Jesus often left the synagogue—the place of worship—to visit those confined to their houses. He entered their homes to bring love and support. We have just shared in worship [*or:* shared in worship on Sunday] around the table at [church name]. You have gathered there with us on many occasions. We know you would have liked to have been with us there today [last Sunday]. We always miss you. Since you were unable to gather with us at the table, we have brought Christ's table to you. We have come to share the love of Christ with you and all who reside here. His presence will be felt as we share together the bread and the cup.

Or:

In Philemon, verses 1–5, Paul wrote these words: *"To Philemon...and to the church in your house: Grace to you and peace from God our Father and the Lord Jesus Christ. When I remember you in my prayers, I always thank my God because I hear of your love for all the saints and your faith toward the Lord Jesus."*

We included you [*or:* all of you] in our prayers as we gathered for worship today [*or:* on Sunday]. All of us in your church family miss your presence in our midst, but we certainly know your thoughts and prayers are also with us. We gathered around his table as we do each Lord's Day to celebrate and remember what he did and means to each of us. We would like to share with you now the bread and the cup.

Or:

Paul in his first letter to the Corinthians wrote: *"Aquila and Prisca, together with the church in their house, greet you warmly in the Lord. All the brothers and sisters send greetings"* (1 Corinthians 16:19).

In the same manner, all your church family and friends at [church name] send you their greetings and love. We, in a small way, represent all of them as we have come to share with you about the Lord's table.

WORDS OF INSTITUTION

On the night on which he was betrayed, Jesus took bread and blessed it and gave it to them, saying, "This is my body which is broken for you." And in like manner he took the cup, saying, "This is the blood of the new covenant shed for the remission of sins. Drink you all from it."

PRAYER FOR THE BREAD AND CUP

We thank you, O Lord, for this bread and cup, which remind us of your great love. We draw near to you, confessing our sins, knowing that we will be forgiven. Amen.

SHARING OF THE BREAD AND CUP

And as they were eating, he took bread, and blessed it, and gave it to them saying, *"This is my body."* He also took the cup, and when he had given thanks he gave it to them saying: *"This is my blood of the covenant poured out for you."*

CLOSING PRAYER, AND LORD'S PRAYER IN UNISON

Dorothy D. France

RETIREMENT COMMUNITY OR NURSING HOME

CHOOSING AND ADMINISTERING EMBLEMS

Serving communion to adults in a retirement community or nursing home setting presents many challenges for those administering the emblems. We are challenged to serve communion to individuals who are variously able, both cognitively and physically. Individuals living in a congregate environment usually represent many faiths and have certain expectations about the communion experience. The traditions that these individuals have practiced throughout their lives and the meanings they associate with receiving communion will have a strong impact on how they interpret the experience. It is best to expect that all those in attendance will be receiving communion.

When ordering emblems for older adults and those with physical disabilities, consider choosing the larger disc wafers instead of the smaller rectangular ones familiar to many Disciples congregations. The larger wafers are easier to pick up and, because they are lighter in texture, easier to swallow. For nursing home residents, consider using plastic disposable communion cups to safeguard against health hazards. You may use the same large wafer for older adults in non-nursing home settings, but with the traditional glass communion cups.

Some nursing home residents are unable to hold the emblems themselves. When serving these individuals, hand them the wafer, and if necessary, place it on their tongue. Vision problems may make it difficult for some residents to select a cup from the tray. Be aware of this potential problem and take the cup from the tray yourself and hand it to them when necessary. In some situations, you may need to place the cup to their lips.

When residents are in wheelchairs, their seats may not form straight rows. Be flexible in serving and make certain you do not miss anyone. In some traditions, residents feel that they have been "refused communion" if you pass by them. Cognitively impaired residents may not understand that you are serving communion. If they appear confused, a gentle reminder "Would you like to take communion?" will help the process. Finally, some older adults may fall asleep. When you reach them, gently tap their shoulder to wake them. They are there to receive communion, and it is appropriate for you to wake them so that they may take part.

MEDITATION

When we close our eyes and think of the things that are most dear to us, our minds may fall back to our past—our home when we were a child, good times with family and friends, the special days when we gathered together around the radio. These are memories that remind us of home. Perhaps it is a feeling now more than a place, but the images still fill us with a sense of peace and comfort.

As we gather around the Lord's table today, as many of us have done throughout our lives, we are coming home. We know what to expect. We know we are welcome. We know we are chosen. The Bible tells us that home is where the heart is. Therefore, if we can bring our hearts, hungry for nourishment, to the Lord's table, then we can see that this is our common home. We are called to be here.

Some of us have said good-bye many times in our lives—to those we love, to the houses where we raised our families, and even to our youth. Yet at this table, we are called to come home again and again. We need not say good-bye to the promise of salvation that awaits us here. We need never let go of the peace that comes to us through this invitation.

As we join together in receiving communion, let us rejoice in God's goodness and mercy. Let us remember that the familiar words and prayers can bring us comfort today, tomorrow, and in the days to come. We are called, we are chosen, and at the Lord's table, we find a common home.

PRAYER FOR THE BREAD

O loving and merciful God, you sacrificed your son so that we may join in the banquet of salvation. As we receive the bread, help us to accept this invitation with joy, ever mindful that we are called to be renewed through the body of our Lord Jesus Christ. Amen.

PRAYER FOR THE CUP

Dear gracious and loving God, we drink the cup as a reminder of Jesus' blood shed for us. Help us to drink with gratitude, knowing that each time we come to the table, we are invited to recommit our hearts and our lives to Christian service. Amen.

Daniel D. Gilbert

HOSPITAL

Administering communion to a patient in a hospital may be the most difficult task a minister or elder is called upon to perform. The person to receive the communion is not only confined to a health care facility, but may be there under conditions that do not always end as one would wish. Preparation for this visit should be made prayerfully and with humility and compassion.

When the hospital visit is made, remember that you are representing not only your particular congregation, but the God you have come to know and understand through the church. Always dress appropriately for your visit.

It is a good idea for elders to wear an identification badge when visiting unless they are accompanied by a minister who is wearing identification. Members of the clergy are sometimes provided with identification badges by the hospital, and many wear a clerical collar that further identifies them and their role while at the hospital. If an elder is visiting alone, a name tag with the individual's name, position held (function), and name of the church alerts the hospital staff to the particular reason for the visit. An example would be: Alice Barker, Elder, First Christian Church.

It is always best to check with the nurse on the unit before going to the patient's room. We think of our visit from the spiritual point of view, but there are other things to consider as well. Your purpose is to introduce yourself as a visitor to a certain patient to administer communion. The nurse can help guarantee the integrity of your time while you are there and in some instances may be willing to be present and assist with choosing the most appropriate location for the placement of the elements.

Consultation with the nurse will also assure that there is nothing about the patient's condition that could be compromised by receiving communion at that particular time. The patient may be scheduled for tests and should not receive food or juice, no matter how small the amount. The patient could possibly be receiving drug treatment that would preclude receiving communion. The patient may be scheduled for surgery and the hospital staff busy with preparations.

Always be sensitive to the condition of the patient. Why was the person admitted to the hospital? Is the patient there for tests, therapy, special treatments, or surgery? What is the prognosis? Has the patient or a family member requested the communion or is this a regularly scheduled visit for hospitalized members by the elders?

The timing of your visit is important. Unless the visit is of an emergency nature, plan the visit later in the morning or afternoon so that it does not interfere with bath time, tests, or treatments. Sunday afternoon after four is a good time for those who may be hospitalized over the weekend.

If family members are present, they should be invited to participate. Most portable communion kits provide storage for elements to serve four to six persons. It is better to be prepared ahead of time to serve family members if they wish to be included. Their wishes should be respected, however, if they decline.

The same care that is taken when preparing and disposing of the emblems in a formal setting should be taken here as well. Wafers and disposable cups are preferable for hospital use.

And perhaps most important of all, clergy and elders should use good judgment when administering the emblems. The use of a wafer is preferred because it is more easily handled and digested. The patient may be in traction, receiving intravenous treatment, or restricted to a reclining position. In certain situations such as the ones named above, it may be best to dip the wafer in the cup and place it on the patient's tongue. If the patient cannot handle solids, the wafer may be broken and only a small piece dipped into the cup. You may also touch the patient's lips with the juice from the wafer in an act of intention. The regular method of passing the bread and the cup to the patient is perfectly acceptable if it can be handled without embarrasing or compromising the patient.

Don't be afraid to touch the patients unless advised otherwise. Holding their hands, placing your hand on top of theirs, or laying your hand on their shoulder as you pray for them often says more to patients than the words you speak.

Most hospitals now have pastoral care departments with paid and/or volunteer chaplains. Feel free to ask for their assistance. The chaplain can help with the initial arrangements or administer the communion if requested to do so. Many will have bread and wine or juice and some will have what is known as "reserved sacrament" available for use in an emergency situation. This is bread and wine that have already been blessed by a clergyperson, as required by many denominations, and thus can be administered by a designated layperson. This is not a problem for Disciples but may sometimes help allay concern when family members may be of a different denomination.

The service itself should be brief. The service given below should be adapted to meet the needs of individual patients. The words of institution, a prayer, and the partaking of the emblems will be sufficient, particularly with very ill patients.

CALL TO COMMUNION

"It is good to give thanks to the LORD, to sing praises to your name, O Most High; to declare your steadfast love in the morning, and your faithfulness by night." (Psalm 92:1-2.)

THE LORD'S PRAYER

(May be prayed by the elder with others participating as appropriate.)

WORDS OF INSTITUTION

We recall that the Lord Jesus on the night when he was betrayed took a loaf of bread and when he had given thanks, he broke it and said, "This is my body that is for you. Do this in remembrance of me." In the same manner he took the cup also, after supper, saying, "This cup is the new covenant in my blood. Do this as often as you drink it, in remembrance of me." For as often as you eat this bread and drink the cup, you proclaim the Lord's death until he comes.

COMMUNION PRAYER

We are grateful, O Lord, for the ties that bind us together as members of your church. You have promised to be with us always and in all circumstances. Be with us now in this place as we come to share about the table with you. Nourish us spiritually as we receive the bread and the cup, which remind us of your everlasting and ever-present love. Amen.

PARTAKING OF THE EMBLEMS

In giving the bread, the minister or elder may say: "Take and eat; this is the body of Christ, which is broken for you."

And, in giving the cup: "This cup is the new covenant in the blood of Christ. Drink of it in remembrance of him."

Or:

When giving the emblems together, such as the wafer which has been dipped into the cup, the minister or elder may say: "This represents the body and blood of Christ, which was given for you. Take and eat in remembrance of him."

CLOSING PRAYER OR BLESSING

May the grace of the Lord Jesus Christ and the love of God continue to surround you that your faith may be strengthened and your burdens eased. Amen.

Dorothy D. France

WORDS
OF INSTITUTION

The recital of the scriptural words states under whose authority the meal is shared. They may be included as a part of the communion prayer, at the time of the breaking of the bread, or as a part of the meditation. The following are all taken from the NRSV.

While they were eating, Jesus took a loaf of bread, and after blessing it he broke it, gave it to the disciples, and said, "Take, eat; this is my body." Then he took a cup, and after giving thanks he gave it to them, saying, "Drink from it, all of you; for this is my blood of the covenant, which is poured out for many for the forgiveness of sins." (Matthew 26:26–28.)

While they were eating, he took a loaf of bread, and after blessing it, he broke it, gave it to them, and said, "Take; this is my body." Then he took a cup, and after giving thanks he gave it to them, and all of them drank from it. He said to them, "This is my blood of the covenant, which is poured out for many. Truly I tell you, I will never again drink of the fruit of the vine until that day when I drink it new in the kingdom of God." (Mark 14:22–25.)

When the hour came, he took his place at the table, and the apostles with him. He said to them, "I have eagerly desired to eat this Passover with you before I suffer; for I tell you, I will not eat it until it is fulfilled in the kingdom of God." Then he took a cup, and after giving thanks he said, "Take this and divide it among yourselves; for I tell you that from now on I will not drink of the fruit of the vine until the kingdom of God comes." Then he took a loaf of bread, and when he had given thanks, he broke it and gave it to them, saying, "This is my body." (Luke 22:14–19.)

When the hour came, he took his place at the table, and the apostles with him. He said to them, "I have eagerly desired to eat this Passover with you before I suffer; for I tell you, I will not eat it until it is fulfilled in the kingdom of God."

Then he took a loaf of bread, and when he had given thanks, he broke it and gave it to them, saying, "This is my body, which is given for you. Do this in remembrance of me." And he did the same with the cup after supper, saying, "This cup that is poured out for you is the new covenant in my blood." (Luke 22:14–16, 19–20.)

[Paul writes:] For I received from the Lord what I also handed on to you, that the Lord Jesus on the night when he was betrayed took a loaf of bread, and when he had given thanks, he broke it and said, "This is my body that is for you. Do this in remembrance of me." In the same way he took the cup also, after supper, saying, 'This cup is the new covenant in my blood. Do this, as often as you drink it, in remembrance of me." For as often as you eat this bread and drink the cup, you proclaim the Lord's death until he comes. (1 Corinthians 11:23–26.)

MEDITATIONS AND PRAYERS FOR SPECIAL DAYS

GOD'S LOVE ANEW

Minister: "Has Christ been removed from Christmas?"
　　　　is often asked.
　　　　The answer is "no" if we don't put him last.
　　　　As Christmas comes once again
　　　　Our lives must be deeply committed to him
　　　　Who came that we might have life and love
　　　　As revealed through him from God above.
　　　　"For God so loved the world he gave his only Son."
　　　　That we might live eternally with him—
　　　　　　all peoples are one.
　　　　Where, oh where, do we begin
　　　　As Christmas comes once again?
　　　　We begin at the manger with God in Christ,
　　　　　　you and me,
　　　　Where we begin our journey to the cross of Calvary.
　　　　One cannot be seen without the other
　　　　For in them both there's the gift of love for us all,
　　　　　　sisters and brothers.
　　　　So with God let us come to Christmas once again,
　　　　Loving one another as we let the Christ Child in.
Elder:　Christmas comes once again.

31

Minister: To proclaim the message of love
         that redeems us from sin.
         But where, oh where, do we begin
         As Christmas comes once again?
People: We begin at the table of our Lord
         where we can be refreshed and repent.
        Where we eat of the bread and drink of the cup
         to experience God's love anew
         in this season of Advent.
Elder: So come, sing, meditate, and pray.
Minister: Open your hearts and minds to the one who said,
         "I am the Light…I am the Way."
Hymn: "Come, Thou Long-Expected Jesus"

Elder: PRAYER FOR THE BREAD

    Eternal God, as we journey through this Advent season, let us be mindful of your gift of love to us through your son and our Savior, Jesus. May he be born anew in our hearts as we eat of this bread in remembrance of his coming and his being with us. May we celebrate his birth this holy season by being Christ-like in all we say and do. Amen.

Elder: PRAYER FOR THE CUP

    For your love, your gift of Jesus, and these symbols of remembrance, we praise your name, Eternal God. As we drink of this cup that reminds us of your redeeming love through Christ, may we too commit ourselves to give the gift of love to others. As we pass the cup from one to another, may your spirit bless us with renewed hope and abiding peace for our Advent journey. Amen.

Richard V. Ziglar

LIKE SHEPHERDS IN ADVENT

Advent means "coming toward something" or "something coming toward you." Capitalize the word, and we are talking about the beginning of the Christmas season. Advent is the most festive of our Christmas seasons. It begins quietly, moving along as in a grand processional, until it comes to a proper worship before the manger.

But it is all so predictable! We know everything that is about to happen. There is no mystery, no surprise. It was not like that on the first "Advent." Do you remember the shepherds, living with their sheep, smelling like sheep, coarse and unwashed, sweating and swearing when the storms struck or an old ewe led some of the flock off and got them lost?

Herding sheep is no fun, you know, like a thousand other tasks the common folks have had to perform for endless days and nights for thousands of years. It's a lonely job filled with boredom so thick that one could almost wish for a storm or the attack of a wild animal or a mild argument.

What do you think they talked about out there in the cold night, huddled in ragged wool? They were not alive with "just a few more shopping days." They didn't say, "You know, the angels are about to sing. We had better brush off the dust and get ready to travel to the manger." No, I suspect their chatter was much like ours as we pass through our daily routines. They complained of the low price of wool, the prospect of a good lamb crop, tiresome spouses, sick kids, trouble with the boss, the cost of living, the weather, thieving politicians, grasping bankers, too much crime, and unjust justice.

The thought of those shepherds a night or two before the heavens broke open over their heads ought to do something for us; perhaps deepen our faith and rekindle our hope. We are like "shepherds" in Advent. Life is always long on Advents and short on Christmas Days. The only reason we get in on any Christmas Day is because we have been out there doing our boring duties for a long time. We never know but what some angel choir is warming up just offstage and out of sight, ready to split the heavens with an astounding announcement.

God doesn't always let us in on the divine plans, but Advent ought to silence the cynic, ease the irritation of impatience, and cast some small glow of hope into our daily routines. After all, his life, from birth to resurrection, is known to us. As we come about this table of celebration, let us be reminded of his coming again into our midst as we prepare to celebrate his birth.

PRAYER FOR THE BREAD

O God of hope, as we move through this Advent season and gather about this, your table, may we, like the shepherds, hear the voices of the angels, calling us to Bethlehem. Send us forth on the journey, strengthened by this bread, remembering your death as we celebrate your birth. Amen.

PRAYER FOR THE CUP

Help us to remember, O Lord, that we are not alone as we come to this table. Generations before us as well as generations to come have journeyed, and will continue to journey, along with the shepherds to worship him. As we hold and drink from the cup, may our lives be open to hear his announcements of peace and joy. Amen.

John R. Saunders

LET US MAGNIFY THE LORD
(Based on Luke 1:47–55)

In the beautiful Magnificat, Mary says, "My soul magnifies the Lord, and my spirit rejoices in God my Savior." She goes on to say, "The mighty one has done great things for me, and holy is his name."

Since we know the "rest of the story," I can't help but wonder if Mary was always so willing to magnify the Lord and rejoice in God.

When she took that long journey to Bethlehem in the last days of her pregnancy, was she still able to say, "the mighty one has done great things for me"?

When her baby was born and laid in the food box of the cows, did she still think this was still such a good idea?

When Mary watched as the king slaughtered so many children, trying to kill her son, did she wonder how so tiny a person could threaten the mighty and powerful?

When Mary stood by the cross and watched as the life drained away from her firstborn, did she question at all the wisdom of God?

How can one magnify the Lord when things look so dark and the end seems so obvious and final?

Since Mary was human, like you and me, I'm sure she was at times weary and fearful, confused and concerned. I'm sure she had questions and doubts that crowded into her brain and heart. I'm sure she struggled with the meaning of this miraculous birth and the agonizing death she witnessed all too soon.

If this is what it means to find favor with God, I'm sure Mary would just as soon have been passed over for the job of bearing Christ to the world.

Except for one thing: Mary had the knowledge that God was with her in a special way. The angel had told her that nothing was impossible with God. Mary gave her life to that impossible possibility.

We gather around a table, knowing that during this season we celebrate not only Christ's birth, but his death and resurrection. God is present with us in Jesus Christ. God is with each of us in Jesus Christ. God is with each of us in a special way through the gift of Jesus Christ. And in the impossible possibility of life coming out of death, we know that nothing can separate us from God's love.

So let us magnify the Lord with Mary. Let us anticipate Christ's birth and let us remember the life and death of Christ. Let us rejoice in a God who has power even over death.

PRAYER FOR THE BREAD

Holy God, you fill the hungry with good things, so we bless you and thank you for this bread. In it we remember Christ's broken body. In it we remember our own brokenness and pray that you will come and fill us with your praise. Amen.

PRAYER FOR THE CUP

Our souls magnify you, O Lord. We pray for this cup as we remember the spilled blood of Jesus. We pray that you continue to look upon us with favor. As we lift the cup and taste the sweetness of its contents, our spirits rejoice in you. Teach us how to remember and depend on the promise of your presence so that we, with Mary, might glorify your name. Amen.

Linda C. Parker

THE CRADLE OF BIRTH, THE TABLE OF LIFE

Oh, sweet little baby
lying in a manger
sweet little baby
come to change the world
with anticipation
with wondrous hope
with stars in our eyes
and longing in our hearts
we wait.
We wait for your birth in our lives.
We, who have heard the story many times—we still wait
aching for that story to somehow dawn afresh.

Come, Lord Jesus, come.
Come, baby Jesus, come.
With your first cries of birth,
awaken us.
Bring to us the vision of a star.
Bring to us hope as in angels' songs.
Bring to us fire in our spirit
sweet little baby
coming into our world
changing our lives.

Ah, there it is.
A small glimmer
just a hint of light peeping through
in the midst of darkness.
Did you hear the baby cry?
Oh yes, sweet little baby
make our eyes to shine
make our lives to shine.

A lowly manger filled with straw
a star with beams so bright
a mother's tear, a baby's cry—
it all comes together in wonder.

But even in the warmth of this moment
there is the shadow of the cross.
Even now as we celebrate birth
we remember the child who grew to be a man.

This little baby child, come to bring good news
he will know suffering.
This little baby child, come to bring good news
he comes to change the world.

PRAYER FOR THE BREAD

Mysterious God, as we gather around this table celebrating birth and life, we take this bread, remembering the Prince of Peace, who laid down his life for our sake.

While we kneel along with shepherds in Bethlehem, we eat this bread remembering Jerusalem, Golgotha, God's great love, and Christ's redeeming presence with us now and always.

For to us a child is born. To us a son is given. His name—Wonderful, Counselor, Mighty God, Everlasting Father, Prince of Peace.

The mystery of this table, the awesome mystery of cradle and cross, fills our hearts. Even now as we listen for the song of angels, hope is reawakened. This is the bread of life. In receiving this bread, we receive the Christ born into our lives. Thanks be to God forever and ever. Amen.

PRAYER FOR THE CUP

God of everlasting love and grace, as we draw near the lowly manger where Christ was born to Mary, the manifold mystery of your love eludes us. We bow in the light of the star and in the shadow of the cross. Here at this table may we breathe in the awesome majesty of the story. The story of surprised shepherds, seeking wise men, singing angels, and a baby's birth all bring to mind how you, glorious God, are born into our lives.

This cup reminds us of the one whose blood was poured out, the one whose life was poured out for our sake. He died that we might live. In this season of giving we remember how much you have given. We have heard the story many times, and yet we still cannot take it in. Your love has no end.

For your light that guides us, for the hope born to us on angels' wings, for your love crying forth from the cradle and from the cross, we do give thanks. We share in this cup of salvation and give ourselves to you once more. Amen.

Cynthia K. Stratton

NEW YEAR'S SUNDAY

DISCONTENTED CONTENTMENT

We are more than halfway through a decade that was described by a leading newsmagazine in 1990 as "the age of anxiety." Just in case you do not have enough stress in your life already, you can now worry about the fact that you are living in a high-anxiety era!

We spend millions of dollars each year on self-help books and tapes that are supposed to make us happy; yet a deep feeling of inner contentment often eludes us. We spend just as many millions on psychotherapy in the forms of individual, group, marriage, family, career, and peer counseling; yet a true sense of well-being often eludes us.

The truth is, confusion, frustration, discontent, and despair are nothing new, because our world has always been filled with much anxiety. Sixteen hundred years ago, Augustine succinctly stated the dilemma of being human: "Our hearts are restless, until we find our rest in You, O God."

In his own spiritual journey, Augustine discovered the same truth about life that the apostle Paul had discovered: *"I have learned to be content with whatever I have. I know what it is to have little and I know what it is to have plenty. In any and all circumstances I have learned the secret of being well-fed and of going hungry, of having plenty and of being in need. I can do all things through him who strengthens me"* (Philippians 4:11–13).

Paul, Augustine, and millions of ordinary Christians have all learned that the secret of contentment is commitment to Christ. Christ is the deep well from which our abundant life flows. Christ is the eternal light who continually ignites our inner flame. Christ is the ineffable peace underneath all of our anxieties.

And yet, a deep contentment in Christ often creates a deep discontentment in us about the destructive ways of our world. The deep satisfaction of God's grace in us also creates a deep dissatisfaction at the dis-graceful ways we humans treat each other.

The deep joy we experience as we follow the Prince of Peace leads us to a very deep concern about the divisive ways of our world. The contentment which comes from our commitment to Christ also creates a discontent that impels us to care very deeply about our restless world.

Jesus embodied a life of discontented contentment as he sought to live the good news of God's love and justice for the entire world. His total commitment to God gave him an incredibly deep and abiding inner peace. At the same time, Jesus' almost incessant conflict with people who were threatened by his message kept him constantly discontented with the selfish, self-serving, sinful ways of our world.

On that same night that he broke the bread and shared the cup with his disciples, Jesus poured out his discontented soul to God until he finally reexperienced the deep contentment that comes only by completely surrendering one's life in total commitment to God. "Not my will, but yours be done." (Luke 22:42.)

May our New Year's communion remind us of the incredible commitment Christ has made in order to bring us a deep and abiding contentment, a gift of peace which the world does not know how to give (see John 14:27).

PRAYER FOR THE BREAD

O giver of life, at the beginning of a new year, we thank you God, for your perennial gift of life, fresh and new each day to the whole world. We thank you, Jesus, for your ministry of reconciliation, bringing peace and contentment to our divided and broken world. May the receiving of your bread nourish our commitment to follow you more fully and serve our neighbor more completely. Amen.

PRAYER FOR THE CUP

O wellspring of hope, we thank you, God, for the unceasing flow of your blessings throughout our world. We thank you, Jesus, for your life-giving spirit flowing through our lives. May your cup fill our lives with contentment as we become a channel through which your blessings flow to others. Amen.

Larry Hastings

What A Morning!

"See, I am sending my messenger to prepare the way before me, and the Lord whom you seek will suddenly come to his temple. The messenger of the covenant in whom you delight—indeed, he is coming, says the LORD of hosts." (Malachi 3:1.)

It was about 450 B.C., and the Jews had returned from their exile. With bold strokes, Isaiah had painted their return as a triumphant procession and the resurrection of Jerusalem as an event that would be honored by all nations.

Reality was something else. There was no grand new nation, no recovery of the golden age of David, no prosperity, no renewal of law and justice. Reality was that the little flock had to struggle for existence against fearsome foes. They rarely had enough to eat. The real Temple still lay in ruins. It was a wasted city. The grand dreams of earlier times to be restored were proving to be just that—dreams!

Cynicism and anger were dominant feelings. Even the most faithful were beginning to ask, "When is God going to show he is God?" "Is God a God of justice or not?" "What evidence is there that God cares?" Even the priests and prophets were infected with indifference. Sure, they continued to conduct services, but what difference did it make? It was a time of spiritual depression made all the more dark by the memory of bright promises.

Anticipation and promise and reality! After all the centuries of celebrating the birth of one whose coming was supposed to change things for the better, the only change some see is for the worse. A "Savior?" We haven't been saved from war, divorce, grief, lust, lies, corruption, old age or crime or anything. "Peace on earth?" We can have peace, providing we lock our doors, keep a doberman in the yard, and a shotgun by the bed. What has changed?

These are the sorts of comments Malachi heard, not from the worldly and ungodly, but from that loyal core of faithful without whom no church can survive. They were the ones who cared and tried, who kept the faith and gave their money and time. "It is vain," they said, "to serve God." (Malachi 3:14.)

Malachi offers another promise. In Malachi 4:2, we read: "The sun of righteousness shall rise, with healing in its wings. You shall go out leaping like calves from the stall." What a morning! Healing sunshine and frolicking calves. It will be a sight to behold. God's new day bringing healing for old wounds and a fresh new Spirit to the oppressed and depressed.

Another empty promise? No. Malachi's morning did come, and it wasn't any easier for Jesus than it is for us. We have just celebrated his birth. The angels sang, the shepherds bowed down before him, and the wise men came bearing gifts. But as we begin this New Year, let us not forget that he had to survive Herod, apathy, greed, arrogance, hostility, and impatient disciples. But the sun did rise, on a cross that stretches out a person's arms like wings—healing wings, healing for the thief, healing for the soldiers, and healing for the crowd. "Father, forgive them; for they know not what they do."

As we come around the table at the beginning of this, another New Year, we do so knowing that in God's new day there is a promise of healing. The sun will rise and shed its brightness if we will but put our trust in him.

PRAYER FOR THE BREAD

Lord God, we pray to you for our little world, our little lives, our dimmed hopes, and our broken dreams. We pray with ancient Christians and with our present church. As we partake of the bread reminding us of Christ's broken body, we cry out, "Our Lord, come" as though you are no longer present. Increase our faith in order that we may know that you never left us, that we are not abandoned, and that every day in this New Year can be a new day with you. Amen.

PRAYER FOR THE CUP

O Lord, our God, whose unfailing love is ever with us, walk with us along the unknown paths of this New Year. We remember the roads you traveled, enduring rejection and heartache that ended in your total sacrifice for us. As we drink of the cup, we do so knowing that your presence is with us now and always. Amen.

John R. Saunders

A CHOSEN PEOPLE

But you are a chosen race, a royal priesthood, a holy nation, God's own people, in order that you may proclaim the mighty acts of him who called you out of darkness into his marvelous light. Once you were not a people, but now you are God's people; once you had not received mercy, but now you have received mercy. (1 Peter 2: 9-10.)

The apostle Peter writes in his letter to Christians who were suffering persecution and experiencing alienation for their faith a wonderful word of affirmation. Who amongst us has not known what it is to question one's value and worth in the face of some difficulty, or just on general principles?

There is no better place to discover and be assured of who we are than at the table of the Lord. As Disciples, "at the table of the Lord, we celebrate with thanksgiving the saving acts and presence of Christ. At the table, we celebrate the institution of a new covenant between God and God's people."

The new covenant, taking its direction from the old, establishes those whom God calls into relationship as the people of God. The old covenant ratifies that relationship through the law. The new covenant is ratified by the death of Christ on Calvary. It is at the table of the Lord that we are reminded of this great truth.

As Christians, we are the people of God. The word *people* in Greek is "laos," from which we take our word *laity*. We are the people of God, the laos, the laity. We are a chosen people; a people belonging to God. Once we were not a people. We had no real identity, but now we are the chosen people of God, with real purpose and meaning for our lives.

Our purpose, as the people of God, is made clear in Peter's assertion that we are not only a chosen people, a people belonging to God, but we are a royal priesthood. Under the old covenant, the priests were a select group of persons from the tribe of Levi and the family of Aaron, who represented the people of Israel before God and offered sacrificial gifts on their behalf, granting them only limited access to God.

When Peter says that we are a royal priesthood, he is referring to the priesthood of all believers. The priesthood of all believers is a basic premise of the new covenant, and it is also what we are celebrating on this Laity Sunday. Every one of us has immediate access to God. Each of us has been chosen by God and called to ministry. All of us have the joy and responsibility of serving God and one another.

The sacrificial gifts that we are to offer to God are the gifts of ourselves in worship and in work, even as Christ offered himself. It is here at the table of the Lord that we are reminded of that!

PRAYER FOR THE BREAD

Gracious God, once again we find ourselves at your table. Not as strangers or aliens, but as your people. We bless now the loaf that is before us, a fitting symbol of Christ's body, that was whole and complete before it was broken on Calvary to make us whole. Bind us together as members of Christ's body so that we might represent him in a whole and complete way. Amen.

PRAYER FOR THE CUP

Generous God, in your loving-kindness, you have called us out of darkness into the marvelous light. Once we were not a people, but now we are your people. As we drink the cup, symbolic of the blood that Jesus poured out to reconcile us to you, may we be reminded of the privilege that is ours to pour ourselves out in worship of and work for you. Amen.

Cynthia L. Hale

WEEK OF COMPASSION

SHARING OF GIFTS

Jesus has said, *"I am the living bread that came down from heaven. Whoever eats of this bread will live forever; and the bread that I will give for the life of the world is my flesh."* (John 6:51.) *"I am the vine, you are the branches. Those who abide in me and I in them bear much fruit, because apart from me you can do nothing."* (John 15:5.)

For Jesus, spiritual growth, faithful service, and nourishing love are intimately related to the bounty of the earth—wheat and bread, vineyards and grapes. When he presents himself to his people he chooses the loaf and the cup. *"This [bread] is my body.... This cup is the new covenant in my blood."* (1 Corinthians 11:24f.)

To align ourselves with our Christ involves engaging ourselves with bread and all that nourishes and brings life to our sisters and brothers and, indeed, to ourselves, for the bringing of life to body, mind, and soul is the mission of our Christ and the whole church.

For the Christian Church (Disciples of Christ), the Week of Compassion has over the past half-century become a holy season each year when we recommit ourselves to our year-round vocation to serve the physical and spiritual needs of God's children in every place, whenever they have been afflicted by war, famine, or epidemic.

Every year we present this generous offering for the relief of refugees driven from their homes; for those who suffer from disasters of nature unleashed in floods, fires, and earthquakes; for those who fall ill and too often die from the epidemics that rage from time to time through the human family; and for the victims of the horrors of war which we inflict on one another, our own sisters and brothers. In all of these tragedies our church is present through Week of Compassion assistance. Christ virtually takes flesh and blood once again to feed, heal, and console God's beloved children in every place, close by and far away, because we have been compassionate and heeded our calling to love.

We do not give these gifts because we are good or because we think they will solve the problems of suffering. We give them because we are the followers, the disciples, of the One who calls us to love one another and who presents himself in bread, and wine, and acts of kindness.

The holy table has always been intimately related to the sharing of gifts. The earliest reported eucharists included the presentation of cheese, milk, and honey for distribution to the needy, as well as the bread and wine, some of which was used for the Lord's supper and the rest distributed to the poor. The church has always taken an offering as it gathers for the meal. The meeting of spiritual and physical needs are intimately related.

When Jesus meets us at the table he asks us to remember the hungry, the thirsty, the naked, and the homeless; when we serve them, we also serve God.

PRAYER FOR THE BREAD

We give you thanks, O God, for the gift of bread. In laying this gift before you we remember our calling to be compassionate servants of your own Son, Jesus. We remember how he has healed the sick, fed the hungry, and loved the loveless. We remember that it was out of love that you sent him into the world to show yourself to us in flesh.

Send now your Holy Spirit upon this bread that it may become for us the body of our Lord Jesus Christ, and send that same Spirit upon our lives as we receive this gift back from you that we may be the faithful and generous servants of your Son, in whose holy name we ask these things. Amen.

PRAYER FOR THE CUP

We give you thanks, O God, for the gift of this cup. In pouring the cup, your Son Jesus shows us his blood poured out for the forgiveness of sin. We have beheld the sin of people left injured, homeless, hungry, and sick, and we have known the compassion of Jesus in ministering to all these in every age. We give you thanks for his compassionate love, which we celebrate both around this table and in daily deeds of loving-kindness.

Send now your Holy Spirit upon this cup, that it may become for us the new covenant in Christ's blood, an offering poured out in love for the healing of the nations. We offer our prayer in his own holy name. Amen.

William B. Allen

Is Christ Still a Stranger?

"When it was evening, he took his place with the twelve; and while they were eating, he said, 'Truly I tell you, one of you will betray me.'" (Matthew 26: 20–21.)

These words of judgment came as a disturbing realization to the disciples who were gathered in the upper room. For you see, they knew that Jesus had enemies from without, but it was upsetting to discover that he might have enemies within. *"Truly—one of you will betray me."* His words shocked the disciples. *"And they became greatly distressed and began to say to him one after another, 'Surely not I, Lord?'"* (Matthew 26:22.)

This question reveals how little the disciples really knew Christ. These were men who loved their Master, but understood him so little. They wanted to fit him into their lives, but they had not learned to surrender their lives for his. Even in the sanctity of the upper room, their failure to understand is painfully apparent. Even at the table, they quarreled as to who was the greatest. Even when Jesus washed their feet, he asked, *"Do you know what I have done to you?"* (John 13:12).

All through that evening their questions continued to reveal how little they really knew about their Master. They said, *"Lord we do not know where you are going. How can we know the way?"* (John 14:5.) *"Lord, show us the Father, and we will be satisfied."* (John 14:8.) Jesus' reply is full of pathos: *"Have I been with you all this time...and you still do not know me?"* (John 14:9).

Twenty centuries have passed, and still Christ is asking this same question of us. It is a disturbing question. If to those men who had journeyed and fellowshiped with him, he was still a stranger, is it not more disturbing that centuries later Christ is still a stranger to those who follow him?

As we come around this table during this Lenten Season, we come with the same question upon our hearts and lives— "Surely not I, Lord?" And the Psalmist's confession becomes ours:

O LORD, you have searched me and known me.
You know when I sit down and when I rise up;
You discern my thoughts from far away. (Psalm 139:1–2.)

But our faith welcomes this examination rather than flees from it, for the searcher of our hearts is the Savior of all.

Search me, O God, and know my heart;
test me and know my thoughts.
See if there is any wicked way in me,
and lead me in the way everlasting. (Psalm 139:23–24.)

Ministering to you in Christ's name, I offer to you the bread of life and the cup of salvation.

PRAYER FOR THE BREAD

O God, as we gather around this table we are mindful of the way that we continue to deny and betray Christ's presence in our lives. We proclaim, "Surely not I, Lord" as we carry out our individual ministries, often with closed minds and hearts. Forgive us when we still do not know and recognize the abiding presence of Christ in our lives. As we share this bread, may that presence be known and felt. May we go forth from this table with a renewed understanding of the ministry to which Christ is calling us. In his name we pray. Amen.

PRAYER FOR THE CUP

As we drink from this cup today, O God, we confess that we have wandered from Christ's call to us. May we be willing in the drinking of this cup to be led back into the presence of Christ and thereby renew our loyalty to him. Through all of our wanderings we know that his love for us has never grown cold. As we gather around his table with those who love him, open our ears to hear his loving call to bring our every care and burden to him. Forgive us as we pray for ourselves and for all of God's wandering children, through Jesus Christ our Lord. Amen.

David N. Jarman

THE TRANSFORMING POWER

During Lent our minds turn to thoughts of sacrifice, and our reflections tend to focus on our own inadequacies and sins. Falling into feelings of remorse, we move toward thoughts of repentance. That is good, but it has a danger unless it leads to thoughts of celebration and joy. The heart of the Lord's supper is joy and thanksgiving.

We rejoice that in coming among people Jesus uncovered the presence of God. Through his suffering and sacrifice he now touches us with the endless mercy of God.

In blessing the bread and cup, we are called to remembrance of the transforming power of "suffering for others," and to remembrance that through God's power in the Resurrection we also have a future filled with hope. The God who brought Jesus Christ from the dead has the power to bring us to newness of life.

Participating in holy communion together we celebrate the presence of our Lord and recognize that we are a part of his body, the church. God has given us to one another, as followers of Christ. Through his presence, we find Christ in one another and grow in God's grace. Thanks be to God!

The words of the institution of the Lord's supper speak of a body broken and blood shed. Bread and wine are symbols of that reality. We eat the bread and drink the cup, remembering that it was the body of Jesus which was broken and the blood of Jesus which was shed. As often as we do this, we proclaim the Lord's death until he comes.

Let us celebrate the victory of Jesus whose resurrection assures us that as we partake of his life we become new persons.

PRAYER FOR THE BREAD

Gracious God, we thank you for the gift of your Son, Jesus Christ, who came into the world as a servant of your love, justice, and peace. Through his commitment to your will he has shown us the way of life that can save us from the manipulation and control of our secular society. We thank you for the gift of such a savior.

Bless the bread and bless our eating it together. Through this participation, give us a new sense of oneness with Christ and with all who claim his name around the world. Forgive our sins and cause us to rejoice in health and wholeness, through Jesus Christ our Lord. Amen.

PRAYER FOR THE CUP

Creator God, we rejoice in all of your creation. You have created all humankind and set us in your wonderful world. You have come to us in many ways, but supremely in your Son and our Savior, Jesus Christ. Through him you have made yourself known to us and opened our understanding of what it means to be a servant of your way.

We thank you for the faithfulness of your Son, who died on the cross and touched us by his suffering and sacrifice. Bless this cup as we drink it. Enable us to be so strengthened by your power that we might follow his example and be your faithful servants in this time and place. By the power of resurrection bring each of us to a new life of servanthood, that we might sing your praise and give you the glory, through Jesus Christ our Lord. Amen.

Wayne H. Bell

JUST REMEMBER

Palm Sunday: one last opportunity to join Jesus on the narrow way leading to death…and through death to life. We know what is coming. Like Jesus, we know what is coming after Palm Sunday. Multitudes crying, "Hosanna!" will turn into jeering throngs shouting, "Crucify him!" The triumphal entry will be nullified by his arrest and disgrace. The shame and agony of the cross loom ahead. Like Jesus, we know that he cannot and will not choose another way.

We know there will be a "Last Supper" four days later. We know a sacred tradition eagerly anticipated by Jesus will end up wrapped in sadness. A fellowship experience with dear friends will be diminished by one devoted disciple's vain promises never to desert, another's uncertainties after all their times together, and finally, a betrayal by a third.

We therefore share a very special privilege with Jesus at this Palm Sunday communion time. We have memories of his last week even before they occurred! Like Jesus, we know what will happen, and we go with him anyway. We come to the table on this special day knowing it must not be taken for granted, as the disciples did. It must not reflect the shallow allegiance of the crowds, the cock-sureness of Peter, nor the ultimate disloyalty of Judas.

Jesus would ask his friends—and us—to remember. He would not be angered by the shallowness, disappointed by the bravado, not even dismayed by the betrayal. Just remember, he asked. Just remember, always.

So we come humbly with Jesus, who, knowing it all, nevertheless gave thanks, took bread, and broke it as his own body was to be broken. He took a cup, blessed it, and poured it out as his blood was to be poured out and said, "Do this with me, do this same thing, remembering me."

Come to this table at this Palm Sunday time. Come and receive. Come and remember. Come with Jesus.

PRAYER FOR THE BREAD

God of our Christ, and God of us all, we thank you that Jesus never wavered in his determination to confirm that he loved us more than life itself. We are grateful that he made believable your unbelievable mercy and loving-kindness, exemplied in his own love that was not canceled even when his body was broken. Like Jesus, we give thanks for the bread, and especially for this bread. We humbly receive it with thankfulness for your love. Amen.

PRAYER FOR THE CUP

O God, we are grateful for his love shared though his blood poured out for each of us. Like Jesus, we bless the cup, especially this cup. Humbly, for there is no other way, we receive the poured wine in remembrance, asking you to bless our communing with you and each other. In the name of the same Jesus who gave his life for the life of us all, we pray. Amen.

William C. Blackwell

PALM SUNDAY

BLESSED IS HE WHO COMES

In representing the Christian Church (Disciples of Christ) in world mission through the Division of Overseas Ministries, I've seen the use of palm branches to welcome visitors in Africa in a way that reminds me of Jesus' entry into Jerusalem. At

Lotumbe on the Momboyo River, a tributary of the great Zaire or "Congo," excited boys and girls stick palm branches in the ground along the path from the river landing to the center of the village, where the houses are clustered around the church and school. The light green of the long sheaves stands out against the darker bushes and grass on the edge of the enormous forest, making a natural decoration for a special occasion. Everyone is there, and hosannas are shouted because the guests are welcomed from a sister church in the name of Christ.

When Jesus entered Jerusalem, it was a joyous occasion, and the palm branches and garments strewn at his feet cushioned the stones of the ancient roadway. As in Lotumbe, people were dancing and waving, singing and laughing. Africans have a sense of hospitality that has made partnership in mission a blessing to all who have shared their friendship. They often personify the celebration of Palm Sunday, with trust in God for the future and thanksgiving for signs that hope will be fulfilled.

When Jesus enters Jerusalem, as when he comes into our lives as the presence of God, it is a time of rejoicing. Faith in him gives us strength to face the challenges and temptations of life. He touches our sufferings with his own suffering on the cross. He makes our struggles for justice worthwhile. He enables us to hope for peace in this world and for life eternal in the world to come. He is Lord, and our spirits are revived by his Spirit. If people did not cheer, even the rocks in the street would cry out!

But when Jesus approached Jerusalem, he wept. He knew that those in power would shut their hearts to him! He knew that as a city prone to violence, it would be destroyed. He wept because cities in our own time would see the homeless sleeping in doorways, children by the millions living in the streets and under viaducts, and men and women with no work standing around smoking fires in the slums. Jesus wept because in the cities some people will do anything for money, from deals in air-conditioned offices to pushing drugs on the corner. When he goes on to cleanse the Temple, it is to cleanse the corruption and injustice of the whole society.

The Lord's supper has a special meaning for us on Palm Sunday, because it celebrates Jesus' victory over sin and death for all people and gives to the church its mission of service and witness all around the earth. People of every nation find solidarity as brothers and sister declaring, "Blessed is he who comes in the name of the Lord."

PRAYER FOR THE BREAD

Beloved God, we remember that Jesus entered Jerusalem knowing that his body would be broken and his life given that we might have faith and be drawn into communion with you. We are thankful for the love that he has shown. We pray for that same love to transform our lives in service to one another and to people in need, that you might be glorified in all we think and do. We find comfort and peace knowing that you are near.

We share this bread with one another because he has made us one body for the sake of your mission in the world. We pray for the forgiveness of our sins and for the revival of the Spirit within us.

Bless the church around the world, especially the church in Africa, where there is so much suffering today. Make us aware of our need for them and for their friendship in one human family, and make us aware of how much they need our help and our understanding. Let this bread represent the need of all people for nutrition and health, as well as our hope in your grace. Through Christ our Lord. Amen.

PRAYER FOR THE CUP

Holy God, on this Palm Sunday we take the cup that is for us the cup of salvation, representing the blood of Christ shed for all people. As Jesus did not turn away from facing death in Jerusalem, give us courage to live our lives unselfishly for one another. On the night he was betrayed, he gave his disciples a new commandment to love as he did, and we pray today that we might be given the ability to show that love to the world.

We remember before you the church in Latin America, Asia, Africa, and the islands of the Caribbean and the Pacific. And especially the churches and peoples of Central Europe and the Middle East, where efforts for peace carry the hope of millions. Have mercy, God of all.

Now let this cup bring us closer in faith to the one who died that we might live. And give us trust and joy in the days to come. We ask in the name of Jesus, which is above every name. Amen.

William J. Nottingham

MAUNDY THURSDAY

Re-Membering Jesus

Over a thirty-year ministry I've shared in many funeral services. Each had its own unique Christian contribution. But one still has a fresh, inspiring, and empowering spirit for me. The service of a minister's spouse was celebrated in the sanctuary as a service of Christian worship. The hymns, eulogy, scripture, communion, prayers, and remembrances were personal, joyful, inspiring. Even the post-service fellowship time shared both physical and spiritual nourishment through the abiding sense of Christian community. The Spirit touched most normal emotions and reason. I felt the deep sense of loss, pain, emptiness, and fear, but more importantly I felt a sense of joy, victory, peace, love, and hope. I could sense even the family members were joyful in the midst of pain.

What was so refreshing about this service? For one thing, it was a memorial service for a Christian leader. Later I learned what made even that experience unique. The deceased person had preplanned every possible part of that human experience. Not only was a clear Christian message proclaimed, but also, for that moment in history, the family was not *overwhelmed* with vital details in a time of emotional upheaval. It was as if the deceased had known the time was coming and wanted to help the beloved faith community experience more joy than grief. What a blessing! In a time when emotions and reason were stressed to the limit, they did not have to make critical, personal decisions which would affect the remainder of their lives.

Christians know that John's Gospel is quite different from the others. One major point of difference is that several chapters deal with the subject of Jesus' departure from his beloved community of followers. It is apparent to readers that the disciples were *overwhelmed* by Jesus' conversations about his death or departure. They could neither contemplate nor understand such thoughts.

One of the most beautiful expressions of Jesus' preparation was the institution of the Lord's supper. We do not usually think of it in relation to death because it speaks of life. Yet, think about it a moment. On the Jewish Passover, Jesus took the common bread and wine, blessed them, gave thanks for them, and said to his disciples, "This is my body and blood. Do this in remembrance of me." (See Luke 22:19-20.) Most likely they did not understand those words or the act of *remembrance* until later, when in moments of feeling *overwhelmed* by human experiences, something unique happened in sharing communion, and they felt the joy of Jesus' very own presence. The post-resurrection appearances of Jesus such as on the Emmaus Road, by the seashore, and in the upper room are typical. It's as if Jesus preplanned the Lord's supper as a way of empowering us to rise victoriously and joyfully from the ashes of our overwhelming experiences.

Whenever and wherever Christians gather around the Lord's table to break bread and drink fruit of the vine in *re-membrance* of Jesus, then Jesus uniquely enters our presence and restores our tired, overwhelmed spirits. In some ways it's like a surgeon who takes a human limb severed by a traumatic experience and skillfully, lovingly *re-members* it to its original source, thus restoring its functional status again.

Maundy Thursday communion is one of those experiences preplanned by our Lord to help us *re-member* him in times of being overwhelmed by trauma, so that Jesus can uniquely return and empower us to become victorious and functional again. Thus, whenever we remember Jesus and all the acts of salvation, we remember that all barriers can be removed, so we can continue the faith journey victoriously and joyfully. Whether during the celebration of a Christian funeral in memory of a beloved family member or the Lord's supper in memory of Jesus, these words of our Lord take on a refreshingly new meaning: "But take courage; I have conquered the world!" (John 16:33). Let us come now so Jesus can remove our sense of being overwhelmed and restore us to life and joy.

PRAYER FOR THE BREAD

Creator God, we rejoice that you understand our human dilemmas. We're thankful that even you learned that words cannot always accomplish what actions can; that Jesus fulfilled in the disciples' midst and upon the cross what words of the law could not. So we not only profess in word that Jesus is Lord, but also in deed by coming around this table as the community of faith. Through the receiving of this broken bread we can now say that once we had heard of you with our ears but now have seen you with our souls. Come, O God of love, and restore our spirits with your Spirit. Amen.

PRAYER FOR THE CUP

O Lord, having experienced grief, failure, and broken relationships, we've often been overwhelmed by their powers.

But in the company of fellow strugglers we have mysteriously experienced the presence of Jesus, who has restored our souls. As we drink from the cup, in remembrance of Jesus, we come again in the hope that, as the branches, we will be grafted to the vine which gives life and joy. In the name of our Lord, Jesus the Christ, we pray. Amen.

Robert L. Bohannon

MAUNDY THURSDAY

He Loved Them to the End

"Now before the festival of the Passover, Jesus knew that his hour had come to depart from this world and go to the Father. Having loved his own who were in the world, he loved them to the end....And during supper Jesus, knowing that...he had come from God and was going to God, got up from the table, took off his outer robe, and tied a towel around himself. Then he poured water into a basin and began to wash the disciples' feet." (John 13:1,3–5a.)

What a different way the gospeler has to show us that "Jesus loved them to the end." In a sense it is demeaning even to *think* of washing the dirty feet of such a ragged band. Yet is it not true that the "servant-leader" is one who is always willing to do first whatever he or she asks of those who follow? The servant-leader models. The servant-leader shows, rather than only tells, what others need to do if they are to follow. Jesus, as servant-leader, not only does this, but does it by leading with love.

It was in love that Jesus washed their feet. He wasn't just trying to make a point. He really did love them. It had been a long, tiring journey from their home territory up in Galilee to Jerusalem. They had traveled difficult roads. They often had nowhere to lay their heads. He loved them—indeed, he liked them. They were his friends, his companions, with whom he had shared the depths of his life. He wanted them to rest, to be renewed, to have a time to just sit back, both to recover from the long road behind, and to be prepared for the far more trying road ahead.

So he washed their feet.

Later, John tells us, Jesus said, "I give you a new commandment, that you love one another. Just as I have loved you, you also should love one another" (John 13:34). From this "commandment" comes the word *Maundy*. Its root is in the Latin "mandare" or "to command." It is this mandate that is the source of the reason and name for Maundy Thursday.

But, you say, you can't *command* someone to love. Love is of the heart, not the law. But don't you see, Jesus had the authority to give disciples then and now this commandment because in washing our feet he had already shown his love for us. The next day he would carry this love to the cross. What greater love is there?

So he is not just ordering us to love each other, he is loving us and then trusting the very character of his love to live in and through us. You see, God's love for us, fully given in Jesus Christ, will die within us unless we turn right around and give it away. It isn't meant just to stop here. We are vehicles, instruments, pipelines, use whatever metaphor fits, but we are meant to carry to others what we receive from God.

Robert McCracken said:

Love ever gives,—
Forgives—outlives,—
And ever stands
With open hands

And while it lives,
It gives.
For this is love's prerogative—
To give,—and give,—and give.

What truth! We begin following our Lord's example by remembering and embodying this love as we serve one another the Lord's supper. At this table all people, including even those who have denied, even betrayed Jesus, are welcomed.

PRAYER FOR THE BREAD

O God, you who are so like a forgiving father and a nurturing mother, we come to you on this day of Jesus' command, seeking to know how to "love one another." Help us to see, O God of life, that it is in receiving your love for us that we will be able to love one another. We approach this table with trembling hearts, because we are so deeply touched by your love for us as we experience it in Jesus. Jesus loved us enough, not only to wash our feet, but to die for us. As we partake of the bread, O God, be in us with love, a love that will turn us upside down: from self-centered to other-centered, from narrow to open, from down to up, from despairing to hope-filled. Thank you, O God, for your love that gives us new life. This we pray in Jesus' loving name. Amen.

PRAYER FOR THE CUP

Eternal God, whose will took Jesus to the cross, help us know that to follow you is to go all the way with you. Forgive us when we take lightly your mandate to love one another. Remind us again that Jesus didn't just say this, he did it. Help us to know that you are demanding of us, for you ask our all. Yet you are also the one who first loved us. You never ask of us more than you have already given to us. Now give us, with this cup, the power to go forth and live your love in every way, even if it calls for our all. In the name of Jesus, who gave his all. Amen.

W. Chris Hobgood

EASTER SUNDAY

FIND A QUIET CENTER

Easter is a high point of celebration. The crescendo of alleluias released from our lips contrasts sharply with the silence of Good Friday and Holy Saturday. Joy, smiles, and symbols of new life stir our spirits and move us to shout and sing praise to God.

But there is also a quiet aspect to our faith that is present and appropriate even amid the crashing cymbals of praise that echo in the sanctuary today. At this table we find a quiet center for our lives.

Day by day there is crisis, confusion, and chaos all around us. So it was for Jesus on the night that he established this meal of remembrance. But he did not succumb to fear. He did not fly apart with anxiety. He did not permit the storm swirling around him to pull him away from the purpose of God.

May we find the center that holds life together at this table. In Jesus Christ we are forgiven, we are accepted, we are loved. Ministering to you in His name, we give you these elements of grace, peace, and new life.

PRAYER FOR THE BREAD

Wondrous God, on this day of great rejoicing, we pray in thanksgiving for the simple truths and ordinary actions that hold our lives together. There is reassurance in the affirmation that we are loved beyond, through, and in spite of our pain and panic. There is depth of meaning in holding bread in our hands and passing it to one another. There is profound satisfaction in hearing the words of institution that invite us to remember and partake. Remind us that before Jesus' resurrection there was death. Before his restoration to wholeness there was a broken body. May this bread of life feed our spirits and satisfy the hunger of our hearts. Amen.

PRAYER FOR THE CUP

Life-giving God, we pour out our hearts before you to-day in wonder and praise. We believe that your promise of new life has been fulfilled. In the symbol of this cup, we experience your grace bubbling up and overflowing onto the dry ground of our parched lives. Thank you for keeping covenant with us when it was not deserved. Thank you for sealing your new covenant with this cup, the symbol of Jesus' spilled blood poured out for salvation and forgiveness. As we drink of it, may our lives and spirits be renewed. In Christ's name we pray. Amen.

Gina Rhea

EASTER SUNDAY

O TASTE AND SEE

I've always believed that communion bread ought to taste good. In the Presbyterian Church I grew up in, celebration of communion was a very special time. Observed only quarterly then, it was preceded by a Thursday evening preparatory service and was taken very seriously. My grandmother baked the communion bread in tiny loaves that were sliced and served after the words of institution, as the minister passed the trays to the serving elders, reciting familiar passages of scripture as he did so. I recall the good taste of that bread.

Perhaps that's why this incident comes to me often in worship. It's the story of the little girl leaning on her daddy's arm during worship and looking at him as the bread tray is passed. "Daddy, is it good?" she asks. And as he smiles and nods at her, he thinks, "I wish I could tell her how good it really is."

In Luke 24:13–35, on the first Easter ("on that same day," we read) two of Jesus' disciples, Cleopas and another whose name we do not know, were walking from Jerusalem to Emmaus. They were sad, talking about all that had happened. Jesus walked along with them and talked with them, but they did not recognize him.

When they arrived at Emmaus, the disciples urged Jesus to stay with them, even though he seemed to be going further. It was while they were at the table together, when Jesus took the bread and blessed and broke it and gave it to them, that their eyes were opened and they recognized the risen Lord. What a glorious moment of recognition that must have been.

The two disciples retraced their steps to Jerusalem to share the news with the others, especially how Jesus "had been made known to them in the breaking of the bread" (Luke 24:35).

On this Easter Sunday, we gather once more, as disciples of the risen Lord. We are invited as followers of Christ to come to the table. One of the things that is really good about this experience is that on this special day, we too are called to allow our eyes to be opened, to recognize Jesus in the breaking of bread, and to share that good news with others.

We have celebrated the Last Supper on Thursday night. We remembered the agony of the crucifixion on Friday. And yet the story does not end on Good Friday. Easter comes, and it has come once more in the life of our congregation. Each of us carries within us the hope that regardless of our present circumstances, no matter the pain and fear, the disappointment and rejection of all the Good Fridays, Easter morning comes. And with it comes the invitation and the opportunity for each of us to know Christ anew in the breaking of the bread and to live out the goodness to which that knowledge calls us.

The psalmist tells us, "O taste and see that the LORD is ___.. (Psalm 34:8). You and I are invited to taste the bread and wine and see how good it is.

As a child half a century ago, I knew the bread was good. Today, on Easter Sunday, as we come to the table to share this feast, let us consider how good it really is.

PRAYER FOR THE BREAD

O God, you who made the earth and its seasons, we praise you for all the signs of new life present among us and in your world of wondrous beauty on this Easter Day. We give thanks for this bread, broken for us anew as the body of Christ this morning. Teach us to taste and see the goodness to which you call us at this holy table. And then send us out to share that goodness with all your children. We pray in Jesus' name. Amen.

PRAYER FOR THE CUP

For this cup of salvation, gracious God, we bring our words of thanksgiving. As we partake of it, spark our consciousness of its goodness and open our eyes anew to the living presence of your son in our midst. And as we taste of that presence, lead us, we pray, by your Holy Spirit, to live thankfully and generously with all those whom you also love. We offer our prayer in the name of our Savior, Jesus Christ. Amen.

William S. and Narka K. Ryan

UNITY IS GOD'S GIFT

The Lord's supper represents the longest table in the world. As Christians gather around this table of the Lord in country churches and cathedrals in America, they are joined by the presence of Christians in China, Zaire, Brazil, Switzerland, Fiji, England, and in the uttermost parts of the world.

The words of institution may be spoken in French or Swahili or Spanish or Russian, but it is the same sacrament that is celebrated. The liturgy and music may portray different cultures and traditions, reflecting the diversity of all God's people, but the one Lord Jesus Christ is present in each place, offering reconciliation, forgiveness, and salvation. At the Lord's supper we experience our unity with all who confess the name of Jesus Christ, the one redeemer.

At the eucharist, or the Lord's supper, we understand that unity among Christians is God's gift. God binds us together in one communion across the boundaries of race, creed, culture, language, and nationality. This unity does not depend on whether Christians who gather like each other or agree with each other. Our unity is rooted in one God—Father, Son, and Holy Spirit—the one who communicates a healing, reconciling love for the church and the world.

In the bread and wine, Christ gives us communion with himself. At this table we do not only recall a past event—Jesus' Last Supper with the disciples—but we experience the presence of the living, risen Christ. The power to overcome our divisions, the power to transform our sinfulness to faithfulness, comes from the cross at the resurrection. Christ's sacrificial love makes all Christians one body, giving new hope to the church and renewing each member.

Thus united to our Lord and brought into the one living fellowship, we go into our world proclaiming and living our unity for the sake of Christ. Every celebration of the Lord's supper sends us to participate in God's mission in the world. As one people in mission, we draw all people into communion with a loving God.

PRAYER FOR THE BREAD

As you called your people, O God, to be a reconciled and reconciling community, give us your love and hope. In the bread, the one bread of heaven, change us and unite us to be a sign of your love for the whole world. Through Jesus Christ our Lord. Amen.

PRAYER FOR THE CUP

Gracious God, you, who gave your Son to be our redeemer, forgive our divided ways. Draw us into communion with you and into loving relationship with your children everywhere as we receive this cup. Grant the presence of the Holy Spirit upon us and all your people so that we may be one with all who confess your holy name. Through Jesus Christ our Lord. Amen.

Paul A. Crow, Jr.

CHRISTIAN FAMILY WEEK

WE GATHER AS FAMILY

"Whoever welcomes one such child in my name welcomes me. If any of you put a stumbling block before one of these little ones who believe in me, it would be better for you if a great millstone were fastened around your neck and you were drowned in the depth of the sea. Woe to the world because of stumbling blocks!" (Matthew 18:5–7a.)

"Twenty years ago," a friend writes, "when I was deciding whether to pursue ordination with the Methodists or Disciples, I agonized for a long time over this decision. I finally chose Disciples, and one of the critical factors for me was believers' baptism. Back then I was single."

Today she is the mother of a six-year-old boy who occasionally sits with her in church. Her son is an active, alert child. He is very bright and articulate, and sometimes she forgets that he is only six emotionally because his vocabulary is so "adult." When he sits with his parents, he insists on taking communion. In spite of their rational explanations as to why he should wait, he is very insistent.

She has often given in to him. He knows that communion is the way adults remember Jesus and how Jesus loved us so much that he gave his life for us. He knows that taking communion is a sign of being a Christian.

She writes, "I want my son to feel that he belongs to this community and belongs to Christ. That's the bottom line for me. My heart tells me this is more important than my rational beliefs, at least in this one instance. I realize that others may disagree, and that this is a real issue for many parents. Some have found creative substitutions for the communion elements and some have children who are not as persistent and can handle emotionally passing the elements without partaking."

Many of us have been confronted with this same situation and have made a similar decision as we came about the communion table.

Jesus calls us to welcome the children. Some Disciples have referred to the communion table as the "welcome table." If it is, how can we welcome children to it without compromising our beliefs or giving in to what we believe is a greater good? Childhood is a time when bones are being formed and senses developed. It is a time of great seeking and learning, a time for the seeds of spiritual growth to be nurtured. Gabriela Mistral, a Nobel–prize-winning poet from Chile, wrote, "To the child we cannot answer 'Tomorrow.' The child's name is 'Today.'"

As we partake of this welcome meal on this [Mother's *or* Father's Day, Children's Day, Family Week Sunday] let us remember Jesus' love for the children and his admonition to adults, renewing our commitment to nurture the children in our midst. Jesus asked, *"When the Son of Man comes, will he find faith on earth?"* (Luke 18:8.) The answer is with our children.

PRAYER FOR THE BREAD

Loving God, you have given us the gift of sharing the bread of life with this community of believers. Help us to remember our children, who believe in you too, and who know the love of Christ through us. As we receive the bread, enable us to find ways to include them as they grow into the body of Christ. Amen.

PRAYER FOR THE CUP

O God, we drink today from the cup of your new covenant with us. We remember the sacrifice your Son made for us, and his love for children. Renew our commitment as mothers, fathers, aunts, uncles, grandparents, and friends, to love each other, especially our children, as you have loved us. Amen.

Susan Spurgeon

It Was a Dramatic Day

It was a dramatic day when the church was born, the day which we now celebrate as Pentecost. Seven weeks had gone by since the death and resurrection of Jesus. High drama was about to occur. A collection of "believing" persons from different backgrounds gathered. The place was buzzing with activity and excited conversation, even nonbelievers were coming to see what was going on. It was as though a tornado had hit, with lightning added. At the conclusion of the powerful preaching of Peter, three thousand united to create the first church—and they took communion together.

It was a dramatic day when this congregation was formed. It likely began with a group who had known each other as believers in other places, plus some who only came to look on— even some nonbelievers. It was a day of high drama, with great excitement and conversation, with communion ware provided by one or more of the neighboring congregations, and with exciting preaching. Many united to make this their new community of faith, gathering together at the conclusion to celebrate the Lord's supper.

It was a dramatic day, too, when one confessed Jesus was Lord and savior, just as had been the experience of those at the initial Pentecost event. There was an air of excitement in one's being among the other worshipers as well. Today as we gather for communion, we should expect the drama to continue unfolding for us, for each other, and for the church universal. That will not occur, however, just by remembering the past. It will happen as we allow the symbols of Christ's body and blood to create in us the will to continue carrying forward his ministry of service. It will occur when we understand that the Holy Spirit is renewing and reforming the church, creating in us a spirit of reconciliation, and prompting us to witness anew to God's transforming power through Jesus Christ.

Suggested Hymn to be used with meditation:

On Pentecost They Gathered
words by Jane Parker Huber

On Pentecost they gathered quite early in the day,
A band of Christ's disciples, to worship, sing, and pray;
A mighty wind came blowing, filled all the swirling air,
And tongues of fire aglowing inspired each person there.

The people all around them were startled and amazed
To understand their language, as Christ the Lord they praised,
What universal message, what goodness was here?
That Christ, once dear, is risen to vanquish all our fear.

God pours the Holy Spirit on all who would believe,
On women, men, and children who would God's grace receive,
That spirit knows no limit, bestowing life and power,
The church, formed and reforming, responds in every hour.

O Spirit, sent from heaven on that day long ago,
Rekindle faith among us in all life's ebb and flow,
O give us ears to listen and tongues aflame with praise,
So people of all nations glad songs of joy shall raise.

(Note: This hymn is found in the new *Chalice Hymnal,* #237. If the music is not available, the text may be read as part of the meditation.)

PRAYER FOR THE BREAD

Spirit of the Living God, we have gathered in this place at this table, to make ourselves ready for and accepting of your coming. As we partake of this broken bread, take our broken promises, our broken lives, our broken relationships, our broken spirits, our broken dreams and hopes and make us and these whole again through Jesus Christ our Lord. Amen.

PRAYER FOR THE CUP

    Eternal Spirit, we partake of these crushed grapes that have taken on new form as juice providing nourishment to the body and soul, with the prayer that you—through the Holy Spirit— will cushion those crushing blows that have come into our lives, our homes, our fellowship this week. Then, having received that help for ourselves, enable us to be persons who in the days ahead will soften the crushing blows for others. We ask this in the name of the Suffering Servant, Jesus the Christ. Amen.

Harold R. Watkins

PENTECOST

INTO AN UPPER ROOM

Into an upper room the risen Christ came through closed doors
to be present with the gathered disciples,
to breathe upon them the Holy Spirit.

Into an upper room the same Christ had come on another night
to be present with the gathered disciples,
to break bread with the promise
that they always would remember his broken body
in the breaking of bread;
and to make a new covenant with them, promising
that they always would taste the renewal of forgiveness
when sharing the cup.

Into this place the same Christ has come
to be present with the gathered disciples,
that we might know his presence in the breaking of bread,
that we may taste anew the forgiveness of sin,
and that once again, we might receive the Holy Spirit,
which unites us with Christians of every tongue.

Jesus Christ invites us all to this table.

By accepting his invitation, we join together
in proclaiming our common memory:
that on the night he was betrayed, our Savior Jesus took bread,
gave thanks, and broke it saying,
"This is my body, which is broken for you.
Do this in remembrance of me."
In the same way, after supper, he took the cup and said,
"This cup is the new covenant in my blood.
Whenever you drink it, do it in remembrance of me."

By eating this bread and drinking this cup,
we become the ongoing proclamation of Christ in our world.

PRAYER FOR THE BREAD AND CUP

Hallowed Spirit,
you hovered over the face of the waters,
and then there was light, and then there was life.

Hover over this table, over this bread, over this cup,
and let your divine light shine on us as we gather and share
these things,
that we might experience what it means to become your new
creation.

As Jesus breathed onto the disciples, breathe on us,
Breath of God.
As he commissioned them with the ministry of forgiveness,
help us to share in your work of reconciling all people to you.

Like the mighty wind that gave life and passion and unity to
your church,
let the strong breezes of your Spirit revive us, excite us, and
unite us
in the love of the Christ who offered his life as a gift for us.
Amen.

Philip V. Miller and Dottie Linn Cook

INDEPENDENCE SUNDAY

DON'T TAKE IT FOR GRANTED

A young man tells of his experience while growing up in
the Soviet Union. He and his father were on the way to church,
but their journey was much more difficult than our journeys to
church. The church had no building and no visible signs of its
existence to non-members. On this day, the church planned to
meet deep in the woods to celebrate the Lord's supper. Why
the secrecy? The congregation of which they were members
was outlawed by the government of the then-Soviet Union.

The boy rode on his father's shoulders through the woods.
The father would stop periodically and rest, so as to not attract
attention, or give anyone the idea that he was headed somewhere. At each stop, father and son scanned the woods for
those who might be following or trailing them—secret police,
guards, or KGB agents. If they were caught at the church service, punishment for the father might range from imprisonment,
to losing his children, or even death.

On that day, there were no problems, no secret police, and no KGB agents. A group of dedicated Christians, risking life and limb, gathered to pray, and to celebrate the Lord's supper. They gathered to recall the sacrifice of Christ in a country where Christians were derided as the "enemy of the nation."

When stories such as these are related, there is a timeless quality about them. For many years, people have come to America for the freedom to worship without fear. And America has welcomed those who have come here for religious freedom by offering a safe place for worship, a place where people are not threatened or coerced due to their religious views. How blessed we are to be able to come to this table, not looking over our shoulders, not afraid of what might happen on Monday morning.

It is important to remember that many people today in other parts of the world are gathering around this table at a great cost. This table exists today because of the One who gave his life that we might live. As we approach this table on this Independence Sunday, remember the freedom which makes it possible for us to be here. Don't take for granted that for which many have shed their blood and for which many continue to risk their lives to make it possible for us to be here today.

PRAYER FOR THE BREAD

Creator God, author of freedom and life, bless us as we come to your Son's table this day. As the bread is broken, help us as a congregation to recall the sacrifice made on our behalf. Alert us to the many broken lives today—broken because there is no freedom to worship, to gather, or to celebrate as your followers. We pray that one day this brokenness will end and all may celebrate around this table in the unity which your Son taught and with the freedom for which he gave his life. Amen.

PRAYER FOR THE CUP

Loving and gracious God, who watches us and protects us, be with those Christians today who do not share in the freedom to come to your table openly and without fear. May the blood your Son shed bind all humankind as one in your love and liberate the opressed from the tyranny which surrounds their lives. May the blood of your Son continually remind us that the freedom to share at this table comes at a cost. Sacrifices have been made in order for us to celebrate today. Let us never forget the price which was paid for us to have this freedom. In Christ's name we pray. Amen.

Joseph S. Roberson

LABOR SUNDAY

The Faithful Work That We Do

The experience of Jesus with his disciples in the upper room must have been traumatic. He knew that his death was imminent. Two of his closest friends would let him down; one would betray him and the other would deny him.

Yet, *"Jesus…got up from the table, took off his outer robe, and tied a towel around himself. Then he poured water into a basin and began to wash the disciples' feet and to wipe them with the towel that was tied around him. After he had washed their feet, had put on his robe, and had returned to the table, he said to them, 'Do you know what I have done to you? For I have set you an example, that you also should do as I have done to you. Very truly, I tell you, servants are not greater than their master, nor are messengers greater than the one who sent them'"* (John 13:3–5;12, 15–16).

As we come to the table on this Labor Day Sunday, let us hear the words of Jesus: *"Do not work for the food that perishes, but for the food that endures for eternal life, which the Son of Man will give you. For it is on him that God the Father has set his seal"* (John 6:27).

It can be frightening when we think of how much of life's labor is squandered on things that will eventually be lost. Jesus inspires us as his followers to reach out beyond material gain to the things that will endure. Such menial work as foot washing causes us to consider Jesus' question, *"For who is greater, the one who is at the table, or the one who serves? Is it not the one at the table? But I am among you as one who serves"* (Luke 22:27).

Labor Day compels us to face the perennial problems associated with making a living and making a life. We often think that the persons who receive the highest wages for their labor are more important and valuable than others. But Jesus' emphasis is not on what we receive from our labor, but the faithful work that we do.

In the Interchurch Center in New York City there is a vivid symbol of the Christian meaning of daily work depicted in a sculptured mural. As workers at the Center stream in each morning, they see figures representing a core of occupations, arranged in the form of a spreading tree of life. An agricultural worker is gathering grain. A mother is preparing food. A construction worker is carrying a bag of cement. A tailor is cutting cloth. A clerical worker is busy at a desk. A teacher is instructing her pupils. A doctor is caring for the sick. A merchant is in the shop. A scientist is in the laboratory. At the center of the mural stands a minister in the pulpit. And summarizing the whole scene is the single overall inscription: "Whatever you do, do all to the glory of God" (1 Corinthians 10:31, RSV).

As we come to the table, let us dignify and honor all who work. Let us give thanks for those who not only labor, but in their laboring serve. May the legacy from the upper room—the example Jesus set as he washed his disciples' feet—enrich us spiritually as we partake of the loaf and cup in the name of the Lord Jesus Christ, who came as one who serves.

PRAYER FOR THE BREAD

We bring to you, O God, the confessions of
By accepting your invitation to this table we hav
choice to accept your compassionate love. As we receive the
bread, we renew and affirm our relationship to you as the Lord
and Savior of our lives. Amen.

PRAYER FOR THE CUP

We are grateful for this act of renewal in our spiritual
lives. Give us grace, that we may discover once again our
strengths and capabilities. As we drink of the cup, make known
to us your will for us as individuals, as well as for the life of the
community of faith gathered here. In Christ's holy name we
pray. Amen.

Carl G. France

RECONCILIATION SUNDAY

THE TABLE OF RECONCILIATION

Two sisters haven't spoken to each other for years because of some minor disagreement; a teenage son is estranged
from his parents because he feels they restrict his freedom;
members of a congregation have "chosen up sides" over the
remodeling of the church building; two countries which peace-
fully shared a border now are engaged in a hostile power struggle.
Relationships, once healthy and life-affirming, can become destructive. All kinds of barriers form to separate persons from
one another.

Some barriers are long-standing—for example, the familiar dividing walls of race, class, and creed present in biblical

days. Recall the enmity between Jews and Gentiles and the bitter hatred of the Samaritans.

Walls still exist today between ethnic groups, between the haves and the have-nots, and between persons of different faiths—also between males and females, between persons of different lifestyles and ages, and between political persuasions.

Walls build up in our families and our community and destroy the wholesome, supportive relationships which give meaning to life. And dividing walls build up in our congregations, often over little issues which turn members against each other. When conflict occurs and is not dealt with in a Christian spirit, it can be so destructive that it blocks hearing the good news of Jesus Christ.

The many forms of alienation present in our world are a constant reminder that we are a broken people, separated from one another but also alienated from God. When we fail to love and accept others, we fail to love God and fulfill God's purpose for the world, which is the reconciliation of persons to persons and of all persons to God.

Reconciliation means to change from enmity and brokenness to friendship, or to bring back together those who have been separated. The need for reconciliation is a theme found throughout the Bible, with references made both to reconciliation between persons and reconciliation between persons and God.

The New Testament clearly teaches that there are to be no walls or barriers in the Christian community. Divisions of race, class, creed, or any other factions, have no place in the life of those who claim to be followers of Jesus. The letter to the Ephesians states that the relationships between those who have been separated from one another are restored through Christ, who *"is our peace"* (Ephesians 2:14). He has broken down the dividing walls of hostility, reconciling persons to each other and to God.

To the Corinthians Paul wrote that in Christ, persons give up their old, destructive ways and become new creations.

"All this is from God, who reconciled us to himself through Christ, and has given us the ministry of reconciliation." (2 Corinthians 5:18.)

This communion table is symbolic of the unity we find in Jesus Christ, whose sacrifice on the cross was a powerful witness to the love of God, which restores and heals and overcomes all barriers, creating one humanity.

PRAYER FOR THE BREAD

Loving God, as we gather around this communion table, we remember the life and death of our Lord, Jesus Christ. The bread, which symbolizes his broken body, reminds us of the brokenness in our lives—expecially our separation from sisters and brothers who have a different skin color.

Where we have allowed any kind of barrier to build up between ourselves and others, we ask forgiveness. We pray for the desire and the courage to reverse the injustices of our world, to be agents of healing where there has been alienation, and acceptance where there has been hate.

May we remember Jesus' words to his disciples in the upper room: "I give you a new commandment, that you love one another" (John 13:34). In his name we pray. Amen.

PRAYER FOR THE CUP

Merciful God, in receiving the cup, symbolic of Jesus' blood, we remember that it was shed by the hands of those who could not accept him. It brings to mind the darkness which still exists in our world because we are threatened by persons and ideas which are different from our own.

Help us to grow in awareness of the ministry of reconciliation to which you have called us and to no longer allow barriers to separate us from one another or from you. May your loving and healing spirit come to dwell in our hearts and be seen in the actions of our lives as we seek to follow your example. Amen.

Marilyn Taylor

The World Gathers

So often these days the church resembles a broken mirror, its many shards presenting to the world a warped and partial view of the Christ whose image it is supposed to bear. In the many expressions of the church there are striking differences in liturgy, in the languages spoken, and in the ethnic constituency, of the participants. How can the church, with such wide variations in its representations, send a message of wholeness to a broken world?

The apostle Paul faced such a dilemma when he sought to establish the church in Corinth. The population of Corinth was an often—uneasy mixture of Jews and Gentiles, slaves longing to be free and slave-owners determined to hold onto their property, rich and poor, educated and illiterate. How could Paul achieve any kind of working consensus among such diverse people? He explained his strategy this way: *"I decided to know nothing among you but Jesus Christ and him crucified."* When Christ is at the center of our life together, all the differences fade away and his hope is realized: *"People will come from East and West, North and South, and eat together in the kingdom of God."*

Cyrus was an important king in the ancient history of the Middle East. There is a story told of him and Caligula, a neighboring tribal chief, who held some land at the Southern edge of Cyrus' kingdom. A border dispute erupted into war, and Caligula was defeated by the army of Cyrus.

Caligula and his wife were brought to stand before the king, to be given the death sentence. Ordinarily that sentence would have been automatic. But something in the regal bearing and manner of Caligula caused Cyrus to engage him in conversation.

"Caligula," the king said, "what would you do if I were to spare your life?" Caligula replied, "Sire, I would return to my home a grateful man, and remain your obedient servant for the rest of my life." "And," Cyrus the king continued, "what would you do it I were to spare your wife?" "Oh, sire," exclaimed the chieftain, "if you would do that, I would gladly give my life for you." So impressed was the king that he required of Caligula only an oath of allegiance and allowed him to return to his home.

A few days later Caligula and his wife were talking about their experience in the king's palace. He said, "Did you notice all the marble walls in the king's palace?" "No," she said, "I didn't see them." He asked, "Did you see all the magnificent tapestries?" "No," she said, "I didn't notice them." Well," he continued, "surely you saw the beautiful golden throne the king sat on?" "No," she said, "I didn't see it." "What did you see the day we stood before the king?" he asked. And she replied, "I saw only the face of one who said he would die for me."

The marble, the tapestries, the gold—the differences of opinion, the diversity of understandings, the variations of tradition—they all fall away when we look upon the face of one who said he would die for us—and did.

So when the world gathers today on this World Communion Sunday, at the table where Christ is the host, all our differences fall away, and East and West and North and South sit at the table together, because he is our peace.

PRAYER FOR THE BREAD

O God, you hold the whole world in your hands; we are all your children. Let none among us feel that she or he is not welcome, since it is your redeeming love that makes us all worthy of being here. In the wholeness of this loaf we recognize the unbrokenness of the world as you intend it to be. In the breaking of this loaf we recognize the fragmentation of the world as it is, and the willingness of our Lord, Jesus Christ to be, himself, broken to bring healing to the world. We receive this bread in remembrance of him. Amen.

PRAYER FOR THE CUP

Our cups are running over with blessings, Lord, which we have neither earned nor deserved, but which you have given us anyway. In our abundance, we think of our sisters and brothers around the world today whose cups are not full, and whose empty stomachs and hearts cry out for our mercy.

In this cup we see the willingness of Christ to drink the cup of sacrifice and sorrow for the healing of the world. Let our participation in this cup bring us together as a worldwide family, which cannot rest until all its children know that they are at home here. Amen.

C. William Nichols

WORLD COMMUNION SUNDAY

THIS IS HIS TABLE

This is World Communion Sunday. Today, more than any other time in the year, Christians feel and experience their oneness and unity in this period of common fellowship around the table of the Lord. Churches of all denominations experience this awareness of one fellowship as the vast multitudes of believers the world over respond to the request of Jesus Christ, who said, "Do this in remembrance of me."

This day began on the other side of the International Date Line in the Fiji Islands, New Zealand, and Australia. Millions of Christians every hour of this day already have been, are now, or will yet be about the table. Those who gather represent many races, colors, languages, and nations.

If we could travel as fast as the earth turns on its axis, we would see one communion service after another—yellow-skinned, brown-skinned, black-skinned, white-skinned, red-skinned Christians, many colors together in some churches, all before his table. Christians from many lands remind us of the length of this table—Africans, Asians, Europeans; persons from Latin America, South America, Canada, Australia, the Middle East, and the United States.

Today Christians will gather about his table, spread with the sacred emblems, in small churches, auditoriums, military chapels, on shipboard, in hospitals and nursing homes, and in stately cathedrals. But even though there are these differences in the kinds of meeting places, Christians everywhere will be bound to Christ by the strong bonds of love and fellowship. Although there will be many interpretations of the meaning of the sacraments, many different modes of celebrating the Lord's supper, the love of Christ is remembered, and our love for him is increased.

Some groups will use fermented wine, some grape juice, and some water. Some willl stand, and some will kneel at the communion railing or altar. Others will remain in the pews and have the elements passed to them. The ministers or leaders will read various forms and wordings for the service. Yet we all will meet the same Christ, who gave himself in love for us. All communicants, wherever they are in the world, will find the truth and freedom that comes from him. In him all things will be made new.

Whatever our denomination, race, or color, far more important than anything else is the act of accepting the Savior as the Lord of our lives. As we gather around this table on this special day, let us be aware of our brothers and sisters throughout the world as they too gather "in remembrance of him."

PRAYER FOR THE BREAD

Almighty and eternal God, we thank you that your love is broad enough to embrace the whole world. We gather in fellowship with your people of every nation and race as members of one family. As we partake of this bread, may it remind us of your body given and broken for the whole world. Amen.

PRAYER FOR THE CUP

O Lord, as we come together about this table, make us truly one in Christ Jesus. Give us a faith which encompasses the world and enables us to join hands with all those who gather at tables everywhere. As we drink of the cup, may it remind us of your blood which was shed, not only for each of us, but for all people of every nation. May your spirit guide us as we go from this place to share your love in a broken and often divided world. Amen.

Dorothy D. France

WEEK OF THE MINISTRY

THE BREAD AND WINE OF MINISTRY

Over the years I have read and re-read Ignazio Silone's book *Bread and Wine.*[+] It has served as an example for me of what ministry is and should be. On this Ministry Sunday, I share my paraphrased and much abbreviated version with you as we think about the bread and wine of ministry.

Silone, who lived in and wrote about Fascist Italy in the mid 1930s, tells of an underground Christian minister who was arrested by the Fascists. A paper was found on him bearing his own handwriting. It said that "truth and human compassion will reign among us instead of lies and hate; servant work will reign among us instead of greed for money."

For this, the militia took him into a courtyard. They put a chamberpot on his head instead of a crown. "This is the truth," they said to him. They put a broom in his right hand instead of

---

[+]Ignazio Silone, *Bread and Wine* (New American Library, 1963), pp.268-270.

a scepter. "This is human compassion," they told him. Then they wrapped him up in a red rug from the floor; and the soldiers beat him and kicked him. "This is the kingdom of servant work," they said. When he fell, they trampled on him with their spiked shoes. The next day he died.

As was customary, relatives and friends came to his parent's home. His father sat down at the head of the table with some of the men. Relatives came from a nearby village. As was the custom, his mother spoke a eulogy for her dead son. She said that after his underground activities and before he was found out, he had gone back to working the farmland, helping his father. One might think he would have gotten tired and disgusted because working the land every day is a chastisement of God. But every morning he woke up his father, he harnessed the horses, he chose the seed, he filled the barrels, and he took care of the garden. Every once in a while the mother paused in her eulogy to stir the fire burning in the fireplace, adding a new dry log.

His father, standing at the head of the table, gave food and drink to the village mourners around him. "It was he," the father said, "who helped to sow, to weed, to thresh, to mill the grain from which this bread was made. Take it and eat it; this is *his* bread."

Some others arrived. The father gave them something to drink and said, "It was he who helped me to prune, to spray, to weed, and to harvest the grapes that went into this wine. Drink. This is *his* wine." The guests ate and drank.

Some beggars arrived.

"Let them in," said the mother.

"Maybe they've been sent to spy on us," someone murmured.

"Let them in! We'll have to take this risk. Many have given food to Jesus without knowing it in feeding beggars and giving them drink."

"Eat and drink," said the father. "This is his bread and his wine."

The beggars began to eat and drink.

"This bread is made from many ears of grain," said the father. "Therefore it signifies unity. The wine is made from many clusters of grapes; therefore it, too, signifies unity." It signifies a unity of humanity, equal and united.

"The bread and the wine of communion," said an old man. "The grain and the grape which has been trampled upon. The body and the blood."

"It takes nine months to make bread," someone remarked.

"Nine months?" inquired the mother.

"The grain is sown in November and harvested in July. It also takes nine months for the wine to mature; from March to November."

"Nine months," mused the mother. She had never thought of it before. The same length of time it took to make her son.

The same time, I suppose, that it takes to make a minister of compassion.

On this day, *this is the bread and wine of ministry!*

PRAYER FOR THE BREAD

O God of Jesus, your Son, our first minister, we come offering thanksgiving for all ministers who followed Christ across the centuries: Peter and Paul, Augustine and Francis, Michelangelo and Bach, Luther and Wesley, Thomas and Alexander Campbell, and Barton Stone, Dietrich Bonhoeffer and John XXIII, Martin Luther King, Jr., Billy Graham, and all the unheralded pastors who have served and loved our congregations across the years. We lift up this day [*name the ministers who have served, ministers who are members of your congregation and those who currently serve*]. Bless our pastor daily and as *she/ he* "breaks the bread of life" for us this day. Amen.

PRAYER FOR THE CUP

As we celebrate the ministry this Sunday around this table and in our separate ministries in days to come, we pray that you join us, O God, in encouraging and supporting our pastor that she/he may minister to us with the spirit of risk, creativity, honesty, and care. As we place the cup of wine to our lips we would keep foremost in our consciousness the eternal, contemporary Jesus, who began his ministry by emptying himself, taking the form of a servant; who carried out his ministry being wounded for our transgressions and receiving stripes that we might be healed. Heal us and renew our lay and ordained ministries in the likeness of your Son, our Savior. Amen.

R. Woods Kent

WEEK OF THE MINISTRY

ALL THIS IS FROM GOD

Here at the table of the Lord, more than any other place, we are reminded that Jesus was among us as one who serves. It was at that table that Jesus set the example for ministry by taking the basin, girding himself with a towel, and washing the disciples' feet. He said, *"Very truly, I tell you, servants are not greater than their master; nor are messengers greater than the one who sent them."* (John 13:16.) As God's "sent" people, we are His servants and thereby servants of one another.

All have been called to share in Christ's ministry, with the promise that we shall be empowered by the Holy Spirit to fulfill that ministry. We believe that this ministry belongs to the whole church, and that all who are baptized are charged with the task of representing to the world, through every aspect of our lives, the will of God for all humanity.

God's ministry is to be received as a gift. God's gifts were that *"some would be apostles, some prophets, some evangelists...for the work of ministry, for building up the body of Christ"* (Ephesians 4:11–12). *"Now there are varieties of gifts, but the same Spirit."* (1 Corinthians 12:4.) The use of the term "servant" and the description of ministry as work makes it difficult to perceive ministry as a gift.

Those who have been baptized into Christ have put on Christ. Since Christ is among us as one who serves, then we should count it a joy to be like him and receive the gift of ministry. It is the gift of ministry that provides an opportunity to show that we belong to one another. Love the Lord, but also love your neighbor, which is a gift in itself.

Paul knew the source of ministry. In 2 Corinthians 5:16–21, where he speaks of our being new creations in Christ, he adds that we have been *given* the ministry of reconciliation and entrusted with the message of reconciliation. He underscores this with a statement that we often miss: "*All this is from God.*" It is a gift from God, not to be received reluctantly out of a sense of duty or obligation, but as a gracious response to what God has done through Jesus Christ.

In 1 Corinthians 4:1–7, Paul describes how ministers should be regarded as servants and as trustworthy stewards of the mysteries of God. He then asks, "What do you have that you did not receive? And if you received it, why do you boast as if it were not a gift?"

PRAYER FOR THE BREAD

Gracious and Loving God, we receive the broken body of Jesus as a gift from one who was among us as one who serves. Strengthen us by the partaking of this bread that we too may serve others in the same way. Amen.

PRAYER FOR THE CUP

May this cup, representing the shed blood of our Lord Jesus Christ, cause us to remember what it truly means to be servants of one another. Amen.

Lester D. Palmer

REFORMATION SUNDAY

RE-FORMATION

Mark, describing the agony of decision Jesus faced in the Garden of Gethsemane, records this "Lord's Prayer." "God, my Father, everything is in your power. Cause this cup to pass from me. Yet not the outcome I seek, but the outcome you intend" (Mark 14:36, author's translation).

The late Paul E. Gary, philosophy professor at Phillips University, envisioned God's response: "God came to Jesus and said, 'Son, the outcome I intend, and the outcome you seek, is the same: that the love I have for you and you have for me may be in these disciples. Is there a better way to show our love than to lay down life for our friends? The cup will pass from you, but only when you drink it.'"

We are invited to this table of remembrance this Reformation Sunday mindful of our need to receive the cup of re-formation. The Christian life is always about re-formation, or change. While not all change is progress, there is no progress without change. When Martin Luther posted his ninety-five theses on the door of the cathedral in Wittenberg in 1517, he sought to reshape the thinking of the church of his time. The cup of re-formation contained the bitter dregs of conflict and pain, which often accompany change. Yet, because Luther wanted what God wanted—that the love with which God loved Jesus might be known in the disciples—the cup of blessing passed from the hands of the ordained to the priesthood of all believers.

Like Jesus, we often pray that the cup will pass from us, for if we are to be re-formed, we must be changed. If we say with James and John, "We are able" to drink Jesus' cup (Mark 10:39), we may be required to reshape the thinking and acting of our church, as Luther was. We may be driven to change the unjust structures of our world. We are likely to need a re-formation of our goals in life if we are to pray, "Not my goals, but yours, O Lord." As we drink this cup of union with Christ, we commit ourselves to the outcomes of God's intention, rather then the fulfillment of our desires.

We gather at the table of the Lord this Reformation Sunday, expecting and celebrating God's reformation of our hearts, our lives, our church, and our world. May we pray with Jesus: "My Father, all things are in your power. May your intentions be done on earth, and specifically in me."

PRAYER FOR THE BREAD

Eternal God of the universe and Father of our Lord Jesus Christ, as the elements of this bread are reformed in our bodies, grant that we may be reformed into the body of Christ. As he blessed the bread, so may we be blessed. As his body was broken, so may the bonds of our sin be broken. In your loving power, as he was raised from death, so may we be raised to newness of life in the service of our living Lord, in whose name we pray. Amen.

PRAYER FOR THE CUP

Eternal Father, whose love enfolds each child in tender strength, make us able to drink the cup of love Jesus poured out for us. Grant that we may drink all of it—partaking of both his love and his sacrifice. Transform this fruit of the vine, that it may reform us as fruitful branches of the life-giving vine that is Christ. May your spirit burst the old wineskins of what has been,

that the power of the new life in Christ might be re
world he came to save. Hear our prayer, in the
risen Christ. Amen.

Jack S. Austin

THANKSGIVING

A TIME OF REMEMBRANCE

*"When the LORD your God has brought you into the land
that he swore to your ancestors, to Abraham, to Isaac, and to Jacob,
to give you—a land with fine, large cities that you did not build,
houses filled with all sorts of goods that you did not fill, hewn cis-
terns that you did not hew, vineyards and olive groves that you did
not plant—and when you have eaten your fill, take care that you do
not forget the LORD, who brought you out of the land of Egypt, out of
the house of slavery."* (Deuteronomy 6:10–12.)

When things are going well with us we have a tendency
to forget the source of our blessings. As our hearts drift from
the Lord, the true source of all our blessings, we begin to feel
that we are blessed because we used our resources wisely, and
made some good investments.

Moses in our scripture told the new generation of Israelites who were about to enter the Promised Land that once they
had entered the land and started enjoying the blessings they
had not worked for, had eaten and were satisfied, to be careful
not to forget the Lord, who had made it all possible for them.

The sad history of these people reveals that they did forget and forsook God who truly loved them.They began to worship gods made by men. By so doing, they forfeited their covenant relationship with God and were expelled from the land.

We, like the Israelites, are prone to forget. Like them, we want to do our own thing. But thanks be to God, we are in a new covenant relationship with God through faith in our Lord Jesus Christ. At the Lord's table we are reminded of who we are, and whose we are. "*But you are a chosen race, a royal priesthood, a holy nation, God's own people, in order that you may proclaim the mighty acts of him who called you out of darkness into his marvelous light." (I Peter 2:9, TEV.)*

The most compelling scene in all history is not Jamestown or Plymouth Rock, but Calvary, where Jesus of Nazareth died on his cross. Here was a man in search of a country—an undiscovered country, the kingdom of God—to which he bids us come.

On this Thanksgiving Sunday, let us enter into the joy of our Lord, which is our strength and our hope. Let us "Praise God from whom all blessings flow." Above all, may we say, *"Thanks be to God for his indescribable gift!"* (2 Corinthians 9:15).

CALL TO THE TABLE

"In this is love, not that we loved God but that he loved us and sent his Son to be the atoning sacrifice for our sins." (1 John 4:10.)
"This broken bread is food indeed,
For my sin-burdened soul;
This poured out wine does slake my thirst,
And makes my nature whole." (John J. Stoudt)

PRAYER FOR THE BREAD

Our gracious and loving God, we truly thank you for your love, which was expressed in our Lord Jesus Christ, who willingly gave his body to be broken for us that we may be made whole. As we partake of the bread, may we be empowered by the Holy Spirit to be more effective witnesses for the church of Jesus Christ. Amen.

PRAYER FOR THE CUP

Almighty God, Father of our Lord Jesus Christ, we thank you for the cup that represents the redeeming blood which was shed on the cross for our sins. We thank you for salvation through faith in the living Christ. Help us to live each day in the sunshine of your love, proclaiming praises to you for calling us out of darkness into your wonderful light. Amen.

THE DISMISSAL

"And the peace of God, which transcends all understanding, will guard your hearts and minds in Christ Jesus." Amen.

Joseph L. Galloway

PEACE SUNDAY

THE MIRACLE OF COMPASSION

Throughout the scriptures of our faith we are told that love is the basis of God's nature and purpose. The writer of John says it most plainly in only three words, "God is love." Jesus came proclaiming God's love in everything he said and did. There is so much evidence for these things throughout the biblical story that we should have little or no difficulty getting it all worked out in proper order. It doesn't turn out to be that simple, however. Somehow a whole world of suffering humanity gets forgotten and left out.

In personal relations and in national and international life we too often let hostility and revenge govern our thinking and behavior. Have we forgotten our compassionate Savior who taught us that compassion makes forgiveness possible, leading us to become reconciled one with the other?

Recently we observed the fiftieth anniversary of various World War II events. We were reminded that one allied raid over Hamburg, Germany, killed more civilians than all the German raids on England combined. And the bombing of Tokyo killed even more civilians than that. Dresden, Germany, was annihilated late in the war even though the city was filled with refugees fleeing the advancing Soviet Army, and even though there was no military target for the fire bombing that occurred. There was Auschwitz. There were Hiroshima and Nagasaki. There was Pearl Harbor.

Are there lessons to be learned from such horrifying events of war? Has it not become clear to us that the barbarism and brutality of war need to end? A start in this direction is possible if we begin to look upon our past enemies with compassion. Instead of continuing to justify and defend the killing in past wars, perhaps sorrow and repentance can lead to greater compassion for potential enemies of future wars. Who knows what force and power that might have on the course of human events to come. One thing we do know is that hate and vengeance lead to a spiraling of hostility.

Our own society today is marked by violence. The National Institute of Health recently named violence as America's number one health problem. Anger, resentment, fear, hate, and despair have created a climate for social disorder. We see this revealed in crime, alienation, distrust, and the breakdown of family and community.

Somewhere in all of this we must find a place for the healing power of compassion, a compassion founded on a realistic understanding of the forces that create evil in society. There are times when compassion will be cursed and despised. Evil always has its proponents and defenders. As Christians we can show compassion for those who are victims of war, racism, poverty, or abuse only if we possess a willingness to challenge those who cause human misery. Did not Jesus set the example for us over and over again?

Compassion will not always bring miracles. In the short term, it may not turn enemies into friends. It may not end hostility or human suffering right away. But who knows what change time may bring. This is why our faith must be strong. We must know with confidence that God is a compassionate God and that Jesus is a compassionate Savior.

As we come about the table on this "Peace Sunday" we must continue to remember the miracles of God's compassion that were seen in the life of Jesus Christ, and be certain that we are called to follow in his way with trust and confidence. The one who invites us to this table was not only called Wonderful, Counselor, Mighty God, the Everlasting Father, but also the Prince of Peace. He calls us now to come with compassion and the desire to work for peace within our hearts and in the world.

PRAYER FOR THE BREAD

We give thanks for this bread, O God, for this simple reminder of the body of Jesus, and for his presence with us here. As we eat this bread may the spirit of Jesus enter into us, transforming our weakness to greater faithfulness.

Turn us from old ways of thinking and acting that cause us to fail to see and feel the pain of human suffering. Help us to really know Jesus, who we remember in this communion bread. We say he showed mercy when others showed hardness of heart. Yet we fail to show mercy and compassion in this broken world where so many people suffer from war, poverty, sickness, and oppression. Come Lord Jesus. Be with us, be in us, and with all who call you Lord. For only then can you truly be present in the world today. Amen.

PRAYER FOR THE CUP

When we receive the cup in memory of Jesus, O Lord, we remember him, and we remember his words, "Blessed are the peacemakers." Accept our gratitude for Jesus, O God, and for his calling us to be one people on earth, bound together in love, as one family throughout the world. We give thanks for all efforts at reconciliation wherever there is hatred and conflict on earth. We give thanks for every act of loving-kindness that nurtures forgiveness, friendship, and community. We know that Jesus Christ is our peace. We know that he is the true source of shalom in our lives and in the world. It is he who has broken down the dividing wall of hostility and reconciled us to you, to one another, and to all people everywhere.

Forgive our sins of hostility and pride that embitter earthly relationships, and lead us to more faithful living through this communion with Jesus, whose living presence is with us as we partake of the cup in his memory. In his name we pray. Amen.

A. Garnett Day

COMMUNION
MEDITATIONS

BREAD: BROKEN AND BLESSED

"On the night that he was betrayed, Jesus took bread and blessed it."

"He could not have taken anything more plain, more a part of common life, than bread. He did not go in search of something strange and mysterious. He took the thing that was right at hand," stated Angus Dun in his book, *Not by Bread Alone.* "He [Jesus] always used the plain things that were right at hand. When he wanted to say something, he took plain examples from the common life of his own time—men fishing or sowing or building a house, children playing in the village streets. He used ordinary words that everyone used."[+]

Bread is our mainstay, our source of energy and nourishment. It is made from the dough of the earth, molded into loaves and baked. Mr. Dun reminds us that bread is not just one thing. It is many things. To the chemist it is a certain combination of elements and the results of a special process. To the working person, ready for a midday meal, it is food, something that we want when we are hungry, something our bodies need. To the shopkeeper it is a commodity, something bought and sold, something that will become part of a family meal.

[+]Angus Dun, *Not By Bread Alone* (New York: Harper and Brothers Publishers, 1942), p. 111.

Jesus took bread and blessed it. He made something sacred of it. He surrounded it with prayer. Jesus took bread and wine, a shared meal, a table of fellowship, and consecrated them. He broke the bread and in breaking it offered his own life to be broken, that the love of God might be shared with you and me. In the breaking of the bread we assemble with others in a community gathered from scattered places to share this meal.

"On the night that he was betrayed, Jesus took bread and blessed it."

Thou art the bread of life. Give me to eat and live. Let us come now to the table.

Dorothy D. France

Gathering About Tables

Let us think for a few moments about tables. This piece of furniture, perhaps more than any other, is the symbol and instrument of fellowship; the bond which binds us together. There are many kinds of tables: dinner tables and picnic tables, card tables and game tables, library tables and office tables, conference tables and peace tables.

We all have a need to belong and be accepted. Gathering around a table gives us that sense of belonging. It doesn't matter whether it is a banquet table or the kitchen table—it can have an extraordinary influence on who we are. It is a sign of friendship to invite someone to your table. We ask friends and sometimes strangers to join us around the table in a restaurant, cafeteria, or the fast-food section in a mall.

The breaking of bread together has always been a sign of community. If you were a member of Jesus' group of disciples, it would not have been unusual to gather for a common meal. "When it was evening, he sat at table with the twelve disciples." (Matthew 26:20, RSV.)

As members of the Christian Church (Disciples of Christ), it is not unusual for us to gather about the table with him. Each of us is a link in the chain of uninterrupted celebration of the sacrament which has never ceased from the Last Supper in the upper room to the present time. Think of all who have shared through the ages in celebration, in remembrance, and thanksgiving.

What happens to each of us as we partake at the table will depend on what we allow to happen. If we allow ourselves to be changed and renewed, we will be changed and renewed. If we withhold a part of ourselves as we come, we will leave only partially filled. Jesus invites us as his disciples to meet him now at this table that has been prepared for us.

Dorothy D. France

In Communion

It was a dream of the ancient Israelites to be in communion with God. But in the Old Testament, this communion is particular rather than general: God promises a covenantal relationship with Israel through the person of Moses. Micah is filled with the Spirit of the Lord. The Spirit of the Lord rests upon Isaiah, whom God has annointed. Israel's hope entailed a belief that in God's chosen time, all the faithful would participate in this intimate knowledge of God: *"It shall come to pass...that I will pour out my spirit on all flesh"* (Joel 2:28–32, RSV).

It is the Christian conviction that this deep, inclusive communion between God and each of us has been established through the life, death, resurrection, and ascension of Jesus Christ and the outpouring of the Holy Spirit at Pentecost. We are in communion with Christ through the mediation of Christ with the Father. In fulfillment of the prophetic hope, the Spirit is *poured out on all flesh* (Acts 2:1–21).

To speak of communion between God and us, the sacraments are pivotal; they are the central point on which all else depends. Through baptism, we become part of the fellowship of believers and participants in Christ's death and resurrection. And the Lord's supper, taken aright, affects our communion with Christ. Indeed, this meal is the symbol of the covenant in Christ.

The table is spread. The body and bread are both broken. The blood and the cup are both poured out. Come and be in communion. *"Come,"* Christ bids us, *"and commune with me."*

David B. Hartman, Jr.

THE UPPER ROOM: AN ORDINATION OF MINISTRY

A little wheat becomes a little bit of bread. A few grapes become a little taste of wine. How commonplace and meaningless they are in themselves. It is so easy to see them only for what they are and what they become and no more. The wheat and grapes carry us back to the beginning of the Christian ministry in a large "upper room" in the city of Jerusalem, where Jesus met with his disciples to ordain them to ministry in a final celebration of the Passover before his arrest and death.

A little bit of wheat becomes bread. A few grapes become wine. Ministers, being and becoming. What a conviction of the Spirit they make possible within us.

A little bit of wheat becomes bread. A few grapes become wine. How deep their significance. For Christ calls us, especially on this Week of the Ministry Sunday, to support ministers in becoming even more than they are. A broken body and blood shed for us—all this in order that our hearts might be broken and opened to God as we realize that his ministry was to die for us.

R. Woods Kent

THE WALK TO EMMAUS

They walked the road of sorrow. As they walked, they talked about the things that had happened to their teacher, master, and Lord.

They talked about his being betrayed with a kiss, about Peter's denial, about the crowd shouting, "Crucify him, crucify him!" They talked about the soldiers leading him away to crucify him along with two criminals, one on his right and the other on his left.

They talked about the Jewish leaders making fun of him and how the soldiers taunted him and how the criminal hanging beside him hurled insults at him. They talked about the darkness that covered them all for three hours and how the earth shook and how the Temple curtain was torn in two from top to bottom. They talked about Joseph wrapping Jesus' body in a new linen sheet and placing it in his own tomb.

They were walking, talking, and venting their sorrow when Jesus himself drew near and walked with them. As they walked, Jesus explained what was said about himself in the scriptures until they completed their journey.

Invited to stay the night, he sits at the table with them. He takes the bread, blesses it, breaks it, and offers it to them. They "eat" and their eyes are opened. They recognize him and then he disappears, leaving them free of their sorrow and grief, free to share in God's new covenant.

Come now to the Lord's table. Come and meet him in the broken bread and the cup poured out. Come and be freed from your sorrows and failed hopes. Come and share in God's new covenant. Then go forth and tell the story of Christ's redeeming love.

Kenneth H. Kindig

LOOK WHO'S THERE

While they were eating... (Matthew 26:26).

Have you ever refused to celebrate holy communion? Have you felt that you were not fit to be at the table? Have you felt unworthy of your place at the table? If these questions have ever crossed your mind, then this meditation speaks to you.

I have read or heard quoted Matthew 26:26–29 countless times. During a recent reading of the text, the word *they* jumped out at me. For the first time I riveted my attention on the participants in this first communion celebration.

In the fellowship hall of our church is a large painting of the Last Supper. With the word *they* reverberating in my mind, I scanned the faces of the persons sharing in this meal. As I focused on each face the words came, "Look who's there."

I see Simon Peter at the table. Simon Peter, who spoke first and thought later, sat at the table. The man who made great promises he could not keep. He would, a few hours after the meal, deny three times ever knowing Jesus. Simon Peter was there!

James and John participated in the meal. A few moments before the meal (through the aegis of their mother) they tried to coerce Jesus into elevating them to seats to his right and to his left. These two, known as the "sons of thunder" because they had not learned compassion, were there.

Thomas, the doubting disciple, ate with him. He had that spirit that is present in every age—"seeing is believing." Jesus must have noticed this doubting spirit long before resurrection morning. Doubting Thomas was there.

Judas graced the table also. John in his Gospel calls Judas a thief. Judas would immediately after supper conspire to betray his Lord and friend for thirty pieces of silver. Later that very evening he would violate Jesus' private praying place and greet him with a kiss of death. Judas was there.

This motley crew comprised part of the "they" that ate the first communion meal. I thank God that they were there.

They represent each of us who gather every Sunday at the table. Look at the faces there. Some have denied him; others have used him for some selfish end. We too have doubted and/or betrayed along the way.

He knows we have done all of this, and still he invites us to the table. What a gracious, merciful God we serve. We are not fit or worthy to come to this table. It is his love for us that makes our seat at the table possible. Thank God that "they" were permitted to eat and drink.

William L. Lee

IN REMEMBRANCE OF ME, "GO WITH HOPE"

Cleopas and his anonymous traveling companion on the road to Emmaus invite us to come to this communion. These two knew disappointment. They knew despair. They knew hopelessness. They knew the sorrow and anguish that came from being abandoned. They knew a sadness so deep that it veiled their vision.

Cleopas and his friend expressed their plight in one terse statement to this "stranger" who had joined them on the journey. Speaking concerning Jesus, they said, "But we had hoped that he was the one to redeem Israel" (Luke 24:21). Every word in that statement rings with the tone of disappointment, despair, dismay, despondency, and defeat.

Have you not felt like these men? Your week began so promisingly. You had hoped that this week you would get a better job, only to lose the one you have. You had hopes that your loved one would get better, but she grew worse and died. You had hopes that Jesus would intervene in your life in some miraculous way, but he did not. As I write this, we have just come out of a prayer vigil, praying for peace—and war broke out. Yes, like the men on Emmaus road, we have hoped and have been disappointed.

Cleopas and his friend invite us to join them at this table, since all of us have hoped and have been disappointed. At this table, our disappointment can be turned to hope again.

This stranger to whom they poured out their disappointment led them from despair to hope. Luke records what happened:

When he was at the table with them, he took the bread, blessed and broke it, and gave it to them. Then their eyes were opened, and they recognized him; and he vanished from their sight. They said to each other, 'Were not our hearts burning within us while he was talking to us on the road, while he was opening the scriptures to us?' That same hour they got up and returned to Jerusalem; and they found gathered together the eleven and their companions. They were saying, 'The Lord has risen indeed, and he has appeared to Simon. Then they told what had happened on the road, and how he had been made known to them in the breaking of the bread" (Luke 24:30–35).

We had hoped.... Come to this table and hope again as we rejoice in the presence of the risen and living Christ. It is into his presence we bring our disappointments; even our disappointments in him. In his presence our disappointments are turned to hope. Let us go forth from his presence with hope.

William L. Lee

A FAMILY REUNION

We had moved three states away from the state of our births, to a place where we had no friends or acquaintances or relatives—or so we thought. As we began to learn the names and backgrounds of the members of the congregation, I discovered that one of the women had the same maiden name as my mother. All persons in the United States who share that familty name can trace their ancestry back to two brothers who had immigrated to the Carolinas some century-and-a-half earlier.

Though we never established where our branches of the family tree connected, I had found a cousin in this place where we had thought we were alone. We belonged to that place and that people because we shared a common ancestry.

That's the way it is when we come to this table. We belong to the same family because we claim as our Savior the one who is the brother of us all. Through his sacrifice on our behalf he has made us all members of one family.

We come to the table as to a family reunion, remembering God's Son, by whom we are called to be that one family. As we recall the stories of our heritage, we also re-member the family in preparation for the ministries of witness and service we are charged to make, so that all people may know their membership in God's family. Brothers and sisters, the table is set, the Host is waiting. Let us celebrate our oneness in the family of God.

Lester A. Ringham

CAST OUT FEAR

"For God did not give us a spirit of cowardice, but rather a spirit of power and of love and of self-discipline." (2 Timothy 1:7.)

In their last days with Jesus, the disciples seemed weak and uncertain. Cowardice led one to deny him. The power of darkness led another to betrayal. As for the others, Gethsemane and Golgotha found them falling away when their presence was needed the most. Unfortunately, the disciples were not able to model for us the traits of strength and self-discipline needed in a critical hour.

Do we display any more self-confidence in our living today? Crime abounds, so we keep our doors shut tight with deadbolt locks. Intent on future security, we shelter insurance policies and heirloom jewelry in safe deposit boxes. We keep precious bank cards and checkbooks close at hand to fund our latest whims. We are truly creatures who relish security.

Today, when we partake of the bread and cup, let us remember that the Jesus of the Last Supper beckons us to set aside all fear—fear of each other, fear of the enemy, fear of an uncertain future, even fear of death. Fear drives out our confidence and trust; and without confidence and trust, we lack the necessary building blocks for right relations and faithful living.

We all long for peace—in our friendships, on the job, and between and among nations. As we come face-to-face with one another around this table, we discover an added dimension to our faith, that in this fellowship is the true condition for peace within ourselves and in the world. In this feast we discover the gift of peace, given by our risen Lord. What happens at the Lord's table opens us to God's spirit of power and love. May this spirit come alive in us today, to cast out our fear and establish peace.

John Shuler

In Loving Partnership

In many of our congregations, people can be heard to say, "We are just one big happy family," or "We are just like family," or "Join our family in worship." Everyone who says this means well and means to be inclusive of all persons. But a congregation is not a family. It is a unique gathering of persons and families who *choose* to unite with each other in a partnership, or *koinonia,* to build up the body of Christ, to spread the good news to the world.

We are born into our families. We have no choice about that. However, we can choose to grow into partnership with our family members, adult and child. Through our love and nurture, we can free each other to serve God by discovering and using our talents and skills to serve others.

We can choose to be or not to be a part of a faith community. We can choose to join a congregation because we see there other persons and families growing into and living out *koinonia*, Christian community, partnership, in their service to each other and to the world.

The apostle Paul said we are all one in Christ. Likewise, we are all partners in Christ, partners with our spouses, our children, our extended family, our friends. We can all be teachers and learners, lovers and nurturers in our common task of building the kingdom of God in our midst.

The Reverend Nancy Heimer, former staff for Disciples Women, often uses the phrase, "in loving partnership." What better way to describe how we grow into maturity in the body of Christ? What better way to describe how we approach this communion table each week?

So let us come to the table with our partners, in one mind, heart, and spirit and renew our covenant in Christ.

Susan Spurgeon

CHRIST'S ETERNAL PRESENCE

I have always appreciated the words of Jesus that boldly stand out on the front of the communion table in the First Christian Church in Bloomington, Illinois. Rather than the usual "Do this in remembrance of me," these reassuring words of the Master speak out: *"I am with you always"* (Matthew 28:20). The meaning of the Lord's table is thus projected beyond the communion service itself to the celebration of Jesus' eternal presence, regardless of the reason one came into the church building.

Whether one has come for personal meditation and prayers, to witness a baptismal service, for a wedding, for an ordination service, for a blessing of little children, for a funeral service, or to celebrate the Lord's Day worship of God—for every occasion, we are reminded that the risen Christ is present.

He invites us to come to him...to learn of him...to grow in faith...to humble ourselves...to love one another...to go into all the world and serve in his name...to remember him as we share the bread and the cup and sense his presence.

As we eat of the bread and drink of the cup, we receive the Christ who becomes the enabler in whose name we can do all things. We share the experience which the apostle Paul described: "It is no longer I who live; but it is *Christ who lives in me"* (Galations 2:20). Let us give thanks for the living presence of Christ Jesus, our Lord, who nurtures us in spirit and in truth each time we commune. By his grace may we be energized to know his will for our lives and go forth into the world to do it.

John D. Trefzger

THE SACRIFICIAL LAMB

Jesus' disciples remembered the Lord's table in the context of the Jewish Passover. Traditionally, the Passover was observed in a home with ten to twenty invited male guests. Jesus observed his last meal in the home of a man whose male servant was seen carrying water, traditionally a job assigned to women, through the streets of Jerusalem.

The meal consisted of sacrificial lamb, bitter herbs, and wine. Mindful that he was soon to become the sacrificial lamb, Jesus no doubt chose this tradition to reinforce what he had told his disciples on three different occasions: *"Then he began to teach them that the Son of Man must undergo great suffering, and be rejected by the elders, the chief priests, and the scribes, and be killed, and after three days rise again.... 'The Son of Man is to be betrayed into human hands, and they will kill him, and three days after being killed, he will rise again'.... 'and the Son of Man will be handed over to the chief priests and the scribes, and they will condemn him to death'"* (Mark 8:31; 9:31; 10:33). They did not understand these predictions; it is doubtful that we would have understood either.

Shortly after the passion drama, the disciples came to see their master as the sacrificial lamb. His sacrifice for their sins reinforced their belief in God and the God of their salvation.

The disciples may also have remembered the words spoken to them by Jesus following the resurrection, *"These are my words that I spoke to you while I was still with you—that everything written about me in the law of Moses, the prophets, and the psalms must be fulfilled"* (Luke 24:44). Today, disciples may well remember Jesus as their sacrificial lamb.

As we come about the table, let us not forget the sacrifice he made for us. May this time together strengthen our belief in God as the God of our salvation.

Thomas A. Tunstall

DO YOU REMEMBER?[+]

The most profound part of our being is our memory. Without memory we would not know who we are. Without memory life would have no reason and no continuity. Without memory there would be no human character because we would not have enough understanding to grow character. Without memory there would be no knowledge, no duty, no love. The

---

[+]Adapted from an article by W. Earl Waldrop, which was printed in *The Christian Evangelist*, September 28, 1955.

scholar would be shut out of the temple of history. In other words, life would have no meaning without memory.

Jesus knew the value of memory when he instituted the Lord's supper. He knew how fickle are the human mind and heart. He seemed to want to establish a special place of memory to which we could come to remember those things that each of us must remember to keep us at our best.

The communion table is that special place of memory. When he instituted this supper, he said to his disciples and to us, *"Do this in remembrance of me."* As you partake of the bread and the cup at communion, do you remember? Do you remember what Christ has done for you when you gather around his table? You should, for that is why it is given to us by our Lord.

Remember that he came teaching that we are the most valuable part of God's creation: we are the children of God. In low moments when you are tempted to feel insignificant and life grows meaningless, remember that each one of us is a child of God and of utmost value to him. The dignity of human personality is a gift from Jesus Christ. As we come to worship each Lord's Day and gather around this table and eat of the bread and drink from the cup, we are challenged to rise above the commonplace plane of life and live on that spiritual plane with our Lord.

Do you remember? He said, *"Do this in remembrance of me."*

W. Earl Waldrop

With or Without Power

There are several familiar words that are associated with the communion service: "This is my body"; "This is my blood"; "This do in remembrance of me"; "Lord, is it I?" These words are of utmost importance and need to be remembered. Also, a few words that are not so familiar can add a new dimension to the Lord's supper: *"I have eagerly desired to eat this Passover with you"* (Luke 22:15).

A few years ago our church was being rewired. The electricity had to be turned off. During that time, in conversations with people, I often said, without thinking: "Our church is without power!" During that week, on Sunday morning, we gathered for worship in a rather dim sanctuary, really missing the lighting that made the beauty of the place more noticeable.

When it came time for communion, without realizing the value and the deepest meaning of the words, I said: "As we gather around this table, let us remember that we have a spiritual power far more valuable than any amount of electricity. We have fellowship with the living Christ!" Nearly two thousand years ago Jesus suggested to the Disciples: *I have eagerly desired to eat this meal with you.* Today, Jesus desires to eat this meal with us.

It is amazing to know that in spite of our fears, tensions, and questions, Jesus does desire to eat this meal with us. In spite of all the many things that separate us from God, the living Christ desires fellowship with us around the table.

As we receive the broken bread, we are compelled to remember the broken body of Jesus Christ. As we receive the poured wine, we must remember the blood of Christ that was shed on Calvary's cross. In the experience of remembering, we share in a fellowship that makes us whole and powerful. It helps us to treasure the fact that we have been created and led and loved by the Almighty who desired that we be close to God throughout eternity.

The fellowship at the table helps us know and experience the joy, peace, wholeness, and power that are available to us; and then we begin earnestly to desire to eat the meal with the living Christ.

Let us prepare ourselves to have a real fellowship with him at this table.

Norman H. Wasson

PRESENCE

It has been the prayer of the "Disciples of Christ" since our beginning on the early American frontier, that here at this table, a table owned by our Lord, we come not as Baptists, not as Methodists, not as Roman Catholics, not as any denomination, but simply come as men and women united and part of the body of Christ.

Today we come as Christians hoping to feel the presence of the living Lord. We come as Christians hoping to be filled with a Spirit that will cleanse our hearts, our souls, our very being.

As we prepare our hearts and minds to receive communion today, I would like to share a story set in the former Belgian Congo, now Zaire.

The weather was hot and dank. No breath of air stirred; leaves hung from the trees as though they were weighted. In the garden not far from the missionary's home, a small boy played under a tree. Suddenly, his father called to him: "Philip, obey me instantly. Get down on your stomach."

The boy reacted at once, and his father continued, "Now crawl toward me fast." The boy again obeyed his father. After he had come about halfway, the father said, "Now stand up and run to me." The boy reached his father and turned to look back. He saw hanging from the branch under which he had been playing, a fifteen-foot serpent.

Are we always ready to obey the small voice of the master? Or do we hesitate, saying: "Tell me why I should do what you ask. Explain to me why I should follow your leading and guidance."

As we come to this table, give us a new obedience to your word and its teachings. Help us, O Lord, to have the faith of this small child.

Jay Waters

COMMUNION PRAYERS

This section contains dual prayers that have been written and previously used by elders, as well as joint prayers for use on holy days and other special days of the year. Additional prayers may be found in the section on "Meditations and Prayers for Special Days." You may choose a prayer that speaks to a particular need or relates to the season or message of the day, adapting it as desired. It may be helpful to check the worship bulletin ahead of time, noting the scripture and sermon topic. Most worship bulletins are prepared near the end of the week and may be obtained from the church office.

PRAYERS FOR BREAD AND CUP

FOR THE BREAD

Almighty God, we rejoice that your Son ate with sinners and that he chose a meal by which we would remember him. What better example of the community of faith could there be than a loaf of bread, from grain raised and harvested by the farmer, ground by the miller, kneaded and baked by the baker? What better reminder of your provisions could there be than a loaf of bread, nourishing grain and oil, the staff of life? What better symbol of sacrifice could there be than a loaf of bread, useless unless broken into pieces and consumed? What better symbol of your love could there be than a joyful meal, shared with those you love, even sinners? Thank you for this reminder of your presence. Amen.

FOR THE CUP

Heavenly Father, when we share this cup we feel eternally wealthy, for we know it represents a spiritual inheritance from you. And yes, Lord, we have not overlooked the symbol you have used: a cup of wine, a gift from you, but a gift nurtured by the gardener, pruned by the vinedresser, picked and pressed by the laborer, fermented by the vintner. Nor do we overlook that this gift of yours is served by human hands. Does this not say, O Lord, that your spiritual gifts of security, comfort, and peace are to be administered and delivered by our hands?

Thank you again for this cup which reminds us that it is a community table where the gifts of God are served by the people of God.

M. Anderson Bradshaw

FOR THE BREAD

Spirit of the living God, descend upon our hearts as we receive this bread. In the quietness of these moments, we come to this table of thanksgiving aware of your constant and faithful presence with us in all that we do and in every relationship. We are aware that you are present, speaking to us of love and sacrifice and ultimate meaning. As we partake of this bread reminding us of Christ's broken body, speak to us of broken bodies in our world today that cry out for the healing power of your spirit. In the name of Jesus, the Christ, we pray. Amen.

FOR THE CUP

God of grace and God of glory, we come now to this, your table, to be fed. We come with grateful and thankful hearts; grateful that we can come in spite of our imperfections and sins; thankful to you for making your love real to us by the life, death, and resurrection of your Son. As we partake of this cup, create within us pure hearts that we may hear your voice. Open our eyes to the needs of the world that, with compassion, we may live out our lives as your servants. In the name of the Christ who empowers us we pray. Amen.

Elizabeth Delmer

For the Bread

Loving Father, it is so good to be here again around your table of remembrance. How blessed we are to be the recipients of your awesome love and grace. As we partake of the bread, we remember that your body was broken for the forgiveness of our sins. Our hearts are moved as we hear you saying so clearly, "Dear child, I love you, I love you. This is my body broken for you." Amen.

For the Cup

Your sacrificial love demands a response from us, O Lord. And so, as best we know how, we want to die with you in our own Calvary. We want to die to self, to pride, to our own plans, and our own priorities. Come and be the Lord of our lives. As we partake of this cup, we pray that our lives will be a blessing to others in your name. Amen.

Bea Harrison

For the Bread

As we come to this hour, knowing that in your love there is mercy, we have the need to own our personal sin and to experience forgiveness. We remember our attitudes that have caused pain to others, and our indifferences to those who were suffering because we neglected to be effective witnesses of your love. As we break this bread together, O Lord, grant that we may receive forgiveness. Let us resolve to dedicate all that we are to the continuing work which you began so long ago. Let our lives reflect your love to all. Amen.

FOR THE CUP

O God of Spirit and Truth, we lift our hearts in praise and thanksgiving as we pause at this table of blessing. May we perceive your coming, humble and meek, into our midst. We are in need of the refilling of your strength to do your will. As we drink from this cup, remembering your suffering and death that you did not refuse, give us a strong determination to fulfill the responsibility placed on us by our master. Bless this cup of life and joy, and grant us the grace to share this joy with others in all parts of your world. Amen.

James and Henrietta Manning

FOR THE BREAD

O Gracious God, as we come to Christ for forgiveness, we all meet at the focal point: the loaf of bread in communion. As we partake of this bread, may we be reminded once again of his words to us, "I am the bread of life." As he shares his life with us so, may we leave this table ready to share his love with others. Amen.

FOR THE CUP

We rejoice in the wonderful blessings that we receive from you, O God. Our lives are continuously filled with your love, even when we don't deserve it. We come asking your forgiveness for the times when we have failed to love others as you have loved us. As we drink of the cup, may we go forth knowing that we are forgiven and accepted through the power of the one who first loved us. Amen.

Barbara and Robert Ozlin

FOR THE BREAD

O God, we come in humility and with grateful hearts for the privilege of gathering around the table to commune with you. We confess that we have often failed to do all that you would have us to do. We have also done those things which were not pleasing to you. We ask your forgiveness. As we eat of this bread, we remember the supreme sacrifice of your Son, Jesus, whose body was broken that we might know forgiveness and experience eternal life. We pray that you will strengthen and guide us so we may better serve you. We offer our prayers in Christ's holy name. Amen.

FOR THE CUP

Our gracious and forgiving God, we thank you for the opportunity once again to partake of this cup in remembrance of your Son, Jesus, the Christ. We are reminded of his precious blood shed on the cross in order that we may have life and have it more abundantly. Let us each examine our own lives, becoming more aware of our selfish attitudes and deeds. As we drink of this cup, strengthen our resolve to follow your leading more faithfully. May our spirits be renewed to do your will. This we ask in Christ's name. Amen.

Marie Pannell

FOR THE BREAD

We are grateful for all the good things which come from you, O Lord—the freshness of the morning, the beauty of each new day, and life itself, which affords us the opportunity to partake of your spiritual blessings. May your spirit remind us that it is easy for us to partake of life's joys thoughtlessly. As we eat of this bread, which recalls for us your son's sacrificial love for all humanity, we call upon you for strength and courage as we give ourselves anew to the task of building your kingdom. Help us to measure both the quantity and quality of our service. Give us the grace to assume cheerfully our just share of the responsibility of making this a better world, after the example of the Christ in whose name we pray. Amen.

FOR THE CUP

O Loving God, we acknowledge that coming about this table is the central act of worship for members of the Christian Church. During this time we feel within touching distance of you. As we take this cup, we pour it out and remember Jesus' shed blood. Our remembrance of Him is repeatedly refreshed by this appeal to our senses of sight, touch, and taste. May it call us to remember the love of Christ, who gave himself for us. We pray in the name of your Son, who died that all who believe in him might truly live. Amen.

Frank H. Richardson

FOR THE BREAD

O God, our gracious host, may the deeper meaning of this communion service never be lost; may this observance never become sterile, ritualistic, or unintelligible. May we remember that Jesus prepared his disciples for his death, and in those last hours he took a simple element of bread and made it a reminder of his last full measure of devotion. How better can we express our own faith than by remembering him through his life, death, and resurrection? During these moments of communion we lift up our prayers for forgiveness. As we partake of this bread, may we find strength to begin another week, praying for a closer walk with you, the source of our being. Amen.

FOR THE CUP

We who are assembled in your presence, O God, and who have accepted Jesus as our master, take this cup which he first offered to his disciples. We drink of it, as they did, as a covenant with Jesus for the shedding of his blood. We pledge here to share with him in the denial of self, and the willingness to forgive and accept the responsibilties and dangers of serving you. As we come before you, we are reminded of the question Jesus asked of James and John, "Are you able to drink of the cup that I shall drink?" Now we ponder whether we are able to face the inconveniences that come to followers of the way: to accept discouragement and even unpopularity for his sake. Help us to have the grace of James and John to say, "Master, we are able." Let this cup be our mutual covenant with him of our loyalty and devotion to his kingdom. In Christ's name we pray. Amen.

Frank H. Richardson

FOR THE BREAD

Eternal God, in the stillness of these moments, we shut out the turmoil of the world and lift up our prayers of thanksgiving. We give thanks for this bread, reminding us of your Son's broken body. Even though we strive daily to live by the teachings he gave us, so often we fail. Give us the courage and the strength that we each need as we strive to share with the world his message of peace. Embrace us with your presence as we share this bread. May it continue to remind us of your great love and the love we are called to share with one another. In his name we pray. Amen.

FOR THE CUP

We gather at this table, O Lord, to reflect once again on that night when Jesus sat and shared a meal with his beloved disciples. We come in order that we may renew our commitment to him and his teachings. Forgive our indifference. Stimulate our enthusiasm to be and do our best. We give thanks for this cup, remembering that it is your Son's gift of his life for us. As we partake, may we do so in remembrance of his sacrifice and love. Amen.

Dorothy Smith

FOR THE BREAD

Bread is often called "the staff of life," a symbol of that which gives us strength of body. For this bread we give you thanks. As we partake, we remember not only the Last Supper your Son shared with his disciples, but also his trial, crucifixion, and ascension that followed. May this bread not only nourish our bodies, but may it nourish our souls so that in times of trial we may have the strength to do your will. Amen.

FOR THE CUP

O Lord, our days are so full of sound and fury. We thank you for this time of quietness when we can be still and know that you are our God and that you continue to watch over us. As we partake of this cup which represents the spilled blood of your Son, our Savior, we give thanks for the lives of all those who prepared us to come to this table. While others may have strived for personal gain, they continued to set an example for us. May our presence here speak to others of our love and commitment to you. Amen.

Thomas W. Smith

FOR THE BREAD

We come around your table, O Lord, today and each Sunday to commemorate the great sacrifice Christ gave in love for us. Open our hearts and minds to accept the strength you offer to each of us. Help us to remember that when we show our love for others, we are also showing our love for you. Put on our lips the words to witness for you and in our minds the knowledge we need to improve the world around us. Now as we receive the bread representing Christ's broken body, we thank you for the promise of forgiveness and the hope for eternal life. As we go from this table into our neighborhoods and work-places, allow us to feel your presence as we live our lives closer to you. In His name we pray. Amen.

FOR THE CUP

As we come to you in prayer around this communion table, we ask that you touch each of us with your love. We each have our own personal demons that try to hold us back from becoming all you have hoped we would be. Our individual prayers also are unique—some filled with praise and thanksgiving for good fortune, others begging for health or forgiveness. Whatever our plea, we ask that you open our consciousness to receive the answers you send. Let this cup be a reminder of his promise to be beside us in all of life's battles. May we take from this time about the table an extra measure of strength to see us through the days ahead. Amen.

Patsy Stockton

FOR THE BREAD

We praise your name, O God, and give thanks for your gift of Jesus Christ as our Savior. We come to this table to eat the broken bread, which calls us to remember that Christ's body was broken in order that our own brokenness might be healed and our sins forgiven. As we receive the bread, we pray for the healing and forgiveness that can come to each of us as we submit our lives to him around this table. Amen.

FOR THE CUP

We prepare now to receive the cup, the blood of the lamb shed on Calvary's cross for our redemption. The sacrifice of your Son is very hard for us to understand, except that we understand your great love for us. We acknowledge that we need that love for our own healing, redemption, and forgiveness. Help us to be loving, patient, and forgiving, showing the same kind of love to others that you have shown for us. As we drink the cup, we accept your love; we accept it all as we make our prayer in Christ's name. Amen.

Jean B. Thomas

FOR THE BREAD

Eternal and loving God, as we come to the table today, we pray that we may be worthy of your love. Create in us a quietness as we meet you here. Give us a hopeful spirit as we reexamine our lives. Guide us as we seek to remove those things that cause us to act with hatred toward one another. Walk with us as we seek to open those doors of service that will guide us to loving relationships. Help us to truly love as Jesus loved. As we partake of this bread, may our minds and hearts be ready to receive his loving spirit. In Christ's holy name we pray. Amen.

FOR THE CUP

Dear God, we are gathered around this table in memory of your Son, Jesus Christ. You know our strengths and weaknesses. As we partake of this cup, strengthen us that we may face the demands of daily life. Help us to experience your strength in our times of weakness and need. As we recall the agony of His death and the glory of His resurrection, may we be worthy of His promise of eternal life. Increase our faith and renew us with a life dedicated to service to you. Amen.

John G. Waller, Jr.

FOR THE BREAD

We gather around the table in order that we might remember the occasion in the upper room when Jesus met with his first disciples, those whom he had chosen to take the message of salvation to a sinful world. We are reminded that this is no ordinary meal; it is a spiritual meal. As we partake of the broken bread, let us do so in calm silence. Here we see enacted again that sacrifice at Calvary which the world cannot and must not forget. When this service is over, may we realize that we are not our own; we have been bought with a price, the body of Jesus, broken for the sins of all humankind. May those who are present today be determined to meet Christ at his table each Lord's Day. We ask this in his precious name. Amen.

FOR THE CUP

As we partake of the cup, we are conscious that it represents the blood of our Lord, poured out on Calvary's cross to redeem a sinful people. When we speak of a sinful people, we are reminded that all human beings are born into a sinful world. There was no one as pure and righteous as Jesus. Open our hearts and minds to the realization of the great price he paid for our redemption. Let us be reminded of the honor and glory that belong to him because of His matchless gift. In his body, the church, we have our life. May the spiritual blessing be real and lasting as we commune this day. In his name we offer this prayer. Amen.

Frank Walters

FOR THE BREAD

We are thankful, O Lord, for the freedom that is ours to worship as we choose. We have chosen to come to your table in remembrance of Jesus. We give thanks for this communion bread, which represents his broken body. As we take the bread, we pray that your presence will be with us now. We ask your guidance that we may begin a new week with renewed dedication to the mission of His church. In his name we offer this prayer. Amen.

FOR THE CUP

Eternal God, we come to the table as a church family, brothers and sisters in Christ. We thank you for the forgiveness that is ours. We pray that you will remove from us the things that separate us from you and from each other. As we eat this meal in remembrance and drink this cup, we pray for the power and presence of your Holy Spirit. With renewed commitment, we promise to go forth from this table to serve you as the Lord and Savior of life. Amen.

Mary Lou Williams

UNIFIED PRAYERS FOR SPECIAL DAYS

ADVENT

O Lord, grant that we may not be so blinded by the artificial glitter of the tinsel, the twinkling of the lights, and the sounds of the Christmas music that we fail to recognize you and pass you by unnoticed. Open our eyes that we may see you as we look into the faces of the children, as we pass those who serve us in the checkout counters, as we approach the homeless who cry out for help, and as we pass our neighbors next door. We pray that as we celebrate around this table, receiving once again the bread and the cup, we may allow you to cleanse and renew us in order that we may truly recognize you as we make our preparations to celebrate your birth. Amen.

Dorothy D. France

CHRISTMAS

For the many blessings of this joyous season, O Lord, we give thanks: the joy of friendships, the blessedness of giving and receiving, and the continuing love of a Savior whose birth we celebrate. As we gather about this table, we express once again our gratitude for the coming of Jesus Christ into our lives. As we partake of the bread and the cup, may we celebrate not only your birth but your life, which was given to become "the good news of great joy for all mankind." Amen.

Dorothy D. France

NEW YEAR'S SUNDAY

Preserve within us, O blessed Savior, a large portion of the Christmas spirit to carry with us into this New Year. Keep us ever mindful not only of your birth but of your example and sacrifice shared about the table in the upper room. You have promised to be with us always. As we partake of the bread and cup, may we be strengthened to enter this new year with renewed faith as we walk more closely with you as our Savior. Amen.

Dorothy D. France

LENT

Heavenly Father, we are reminded that the bread and cup represent the broken body and shed blood of your son, Jesus Christ. In the weeks before his death, not even the specter of the cross could cause his faith to waiver. As we move into the Lenten season, give us the honesty to examine what lies within our hearts and minds that separates us from you so that our own faith may be renewed. We have been greatly blessed by your love. Teach us to share that gift freely with others. We ask this in the name of our Lord, Jesus Christ. Amen.

Patsy Stockton

PALM SUNDAY

It is easier, Lord Jesus, to cry out our hosannas than it is to share with you during the rest of this Holy Week. As we come to this table and receive the bread and the cup, we pray for the faith and courage to share with you in the upper room, pray with you in the garden, and stand beside you as you endure the cross for our sake. Amen.

Dorothy D. France

MAUNDY THURSDAY

Give us, O Lord, a sense of what happened in the upper room as you shared the Passover meal with your disciples. Forgive us that we have been so careless about its meaning and your great love for us. Breathe your spirit through us now as we receive the bread and cup. May we feel your presence in and among us. As we leave this table, send us forth with grateful hearts and lives made whole through your sacrifice. Amen.

Dorothy D. France

EASTER

As we gather around the table on this resurrection morning, we do so with renewed joy and living hope. We are grateful for the gift of new birth that is ours to claim as we partake of the bread and cup. Keep alive within us, O risen Lord, the faith that we share today. Strengthen us that we may continue as your messengers of hope. Amen.

Dorothy D. France

PENTECOST

Heavenly Father, with the Easter season we celebrated Christ's resurrection from the tomb and his appearance to the disciples. We are mindful today of the purpose of that act. The risen Christ empowered those who gathered about the cross and at the open tomb to form the early church. As we partake of the bread and the cup representing the body and blood of our Lord, we pray for his guidance in our own efforts as we seek to carry your love to others throughout the world. In Christ's name we pray. Amen.

Patsy Stockton

WORLD COMMUNION SUNDAY

Almighty and Eternal God, we thank you that your love is broad enough to embrace the whole world, yet personal enough to reach out to each one of us. Within the circle of that love we gather about this table in fellowship with all your children of every nation and race as members of one family. As we receive the bread and the cup, remind us that your body was broken and your blood was shed for all people everywhere. Remind us that each time we gather, we eat the bread and drink the cup with our neighbors here and around the world. Amen.

Dorothy D. France

THANKSGIVING

Help us, O Lord, on this day of gratitude to remember and celebrate the lives of those who have given so much in order that we might enjoy the bounty of the harvest. Above all, we express our gratitude to you for your wonderful goodness and mercy. As we partake of the bread and cup, we remember your body broken in sacrificial love and your blood poured out for the forgiveness of our sins. We pray that we may express our thankfulness as we share your love and compassion with others. In Christ's name we pray. Amen.

Dorothy France

ADDITIONAL RESOURCES

Cartwright, Colbert S., *Candles of Grace: Disciples Worship in Perspective* (St. Louis: Chalice Press, 1992).

_____ , *People of the Chalice* (St. Louis: CBP Press, 1987).

_____ , and O. I. Cricket Harrison, eds., *Chalice Worship* (St. Louis: Chalice Press, 1997).

Christensen, James L., *Communion Reflections and Prayers* (St. Louis: CBP Press, 1985).

Dixon, Michael E., *Bread of Blessing, Cup of Hope* (St. Louis: CBP Press, 1987).

Harrison, Russell F., *More Brief Prayers for Bread and Cup* (St. Louis: CBP Press, 1986).

Jeter, Joseph R., Jr., *Re/Membering: Meditations and Sermons for the Table of Jesus Christ* (St. Louis: Chalice Press, 1996).

McAvoy, Jane, ed., *Table Talk: Resource for the Communion Meal* (St. Louis: Chalice Press, 1993).

Merrick, Daniel B., and David P. Polk, eds., *Chalice Hymnal,* (St. Louis: Chalice Press, 1995).

Morgan, Peter M., *Disciples Eldership: A Quest for Identity and Ministry* (St. Louis: CBP Press, 1986).

Toulouse, Mark G., *Joined in Discipleship: The Shaping of Contemporary Disciples Identity*, revised and expanded edition (St. Louis: Chalice Press, 1997), ch. 6: "The Sacraments."

Watkins, Keith, *Celebrate with Thanksgiving: Patterns of Prayer at the Communion Table* (St. Louis: Chalice Press, 1991).

_____ , ed., *Thankful Praise* (St. Louis: CBP Press, 1987).

INDEX OF CONTRIBUTORS

Allen, William B.—regional minister of the Christian Church in West Virginia, Parkersburg, West Virginia.

Austin, Jack S.—minister of Diamond Springs Christian Church in Virginia Beach, Virginia.

Bell, Wayne H.—president emeritus of Lexington Theological Seminary, Lexington, Kentucky.

Blackwell, William C.—retired minister, former major gifts director of Embrace the Future, Brandywine, West Virginia.

Bohannon, Robert L.—minister, Chester, Virginia.

Bradshaw, Andrew—elder, lawyer, Toano, Virginia.

Cook, Dottie Linn—associate minister of South Hills Christian Church in Fort Worth, Texas.

Crow, Paul A., Jr.—president of the Council on Christian Unity, Indianapolis, Indiana.

Day, A. Garnett—retired from the Division of Homeland Ministries, Indianapolis, Indiana.

Delmar, Elizabeth—elder, retired federal government employee, Deltaville, Virginia.

France, Carl G.—retired minister and consultant on death and dying, Fairlawn, Ohio.

France, Dorothy D.—retired minister and teacher, Fairlawn, Ohio.

Galloway, Joseph L.—retired minister and principal, Chatham, Virginia.

Gilbert, Daniel D.—president, Christian Church Homes of Kentucky, Louisville, Kentucky.

Hale, Cynthia L.—minister of Ray of Hope Christian Church, Atlanta, Georgia.

Harrison, Bea—elder, retired teacher, Hopewell, Virginia.

Hartman, David B.—minister of Harrodsburg Christian Church, Harrodsburg, Kentucky.

Hastings, Larry—minister of Park Street Christian Church, Charlottesville, Virginia.

Hobgood, W. Chris—regional minister of the Christian Church Capital Area, Chevy Chase, Maryland.

Jarman, David N.—minister of Richmond Hills Christian Church, Fort Worth, Texas.

Kent, R. Woods—retired minister, Decatur, Georgia.

Kindig, Kenneth H.—retired minister, Ravenna, Ohio.

Lee, William L.—minister of Loudon Avenue Christian Church in Roanoke, Virginia.

Manning, Henrietta—elder, volunteer in refugee resettlement, Blue Ridge, Virginia.

Manning, James—elder, retired federal government employee, Blue Ridge, Virginia.

Miller, Philip V.—minister of South Hills Christian Church in Fort Worth, Texas.

Morgan, Peter M.—president of the Disciples of Christ Historical Society, Nashville, Tennessee.

Nichols, C. William—retired minister, general minister emeritus of the Christian Church (Disciples of Christ), now living in Decatur, Illinois.

Nottingham, William J.—immediate past president of the Division of Overseas Ministries, Indianapolis, Indiana.

Ozlin, Barbara—elder, nurse, Chester, Virginia.

Ozlin, Robert—elder, engineer, Chester, Virginia.

Palmer, Lester D.—immediate past president of the Pension Fund, Indianapolis, Indiana.

Pannell, Marie—elder, retired elementary school teacher, Fairlawn, Virginia.

Parker, Linda C.—associate minister of Vine Street Christian Church, Nashville, Tennessee.

Rhea, Gina—minister of First Christian Church, Radford, Virginia.

Richardson, Frank D.—elder, retired banker, Richmond, Virginia.

Ringham, Lester A.—retired minister, New Albany, Indiana.

Roberson, Joseph S.—minister, Virginia Council of Churches, Richmond, Virginia.

Ryan, Narka K.—retired minister, Baltimore, Maryland.

Ryan, William S.—retired minister, Baltimore, Maryland.

Saunders, John R.—retired minister, Gainesville, Georgia.

Shuler, John—elder, education and counseling service, Nashville, Tennessee.

Smith, Dorothy—elder, retired office manager, Richmond, Virginia.

Smith, Thomas W.—elder, retired architect, Richmond, Virginia.

Spurgeon, Susan—minister, Springfield, Virginia.